T0311711

Cambridge Elements ☰

Elements in Religion in Late Antiquity
edited by
Andrew S. Jacobs
Harvard Divinity School

MONASTICISM AND THE CITY IN LATE ANTIQUITY AND THE EARLY MIDDLE AGES

Mateusz Fafinski
University of Erfurt

Jakob Riemenschneider
University of Innsbruck

CAMBRIDGE
UNIVERSITY PRESS

CAMBRIDGE
UNIVERSITY PRESS

Shaftesbury Road, Cambridge CB2 8EA, United Kingdom

One Liberty Plaza, 20th Floor, New York, NY 10006, USA

477 Williamstown Road, Port Melbourne, VIC 3207, Australia

314–321, 3rd Floor, Plot 3, Splendor Forum, Jasola District Centre,
New Delhi – 110025, India

103 Penang Road, #05–06/07, Visioncrest Commercial, Singapore 238467

Cambridge University Press is part of Cambridge University Press & Assessment,
a department of the University of Cambridge.

We share the University's mission to contribute to society through the pursuit of
education, learning and research at the highest international levels of excellence.

www.cambridge.org
Information on this title: www.cambridge.org/9781108984485

DOI: 10.1017/9781108989312

First published 2023

A catalogue record for this publication is available from the British Library.

ISBN 978-1-108-98448-5 Paperback
ISSN 2633-8602 (online)
ISSN 2633-8599 (print)

Cambridge University Press & Assessment has no responsibility for the persistence
or accuracy of URLs for external or third-party internet websites referred to in this
publication and does not guarantee that any content on such websites is, or will
remain, accurate or appropriate.

Monasticism and the City in Late Antiquity and the Early Middle Ages

Elements in Religion in Late Antiquity

DOI: 10.1017/9781108989312
First published online: April 2023

Mateusz Fafinski
University of Erfurt

Jakob Riemenschneider
University of Innsbruck

Author for correspondence: Mateusz Fafinski, mateusz.fafinski@uni-erfurt.de

Abstract: This Element will re-evaluate the relationship between monasticism and the city in Late Antiquity and the Early Middle Ages in the period 300–700 in both the post-Roman West and the eastern Mediterranean, putting these areas in conversation. Building on recent scholarship on the nature of late antique urbanism, the authors observe that the links between late antique Christian thought and the late and post-Roman urban space were far more relevant to the everyday practice of monasticism than previously assumed. By comparing Latin, Greek, and Syriac sources, the authors gain a bird's-eye view on the enduring importance of urbanism in a late antique, afroeurasian monastic world.

Keywords: monasticism, city, movements, urbanism, global Middle Ages

ISBNs: 9781108984485 (PB), 9781108989312 (OC)
ISSNs: 2633-8602 (online), 2633-8599 (print)

Contents

Introduction

Monasticism flourished in a variety of forms and landscapes. Between the third and the eighth century it took root in environments as diverse as the rolling hills of northern England and the valley of the Nile. Each of these microcosms tells a different, if connected, story about nuns and monks, their concerns and their lives. But one surrounding, one geographical setting, proved to be crucial: monasticism as a social movement was dependent on its success in the urban landscape. The role of the city in monasticism goes a long way to explain the movement's astonishing success in Late Antiquity and the Early Middle Ages. Theirs was not an easy marriage, a union marked with friction. Monks and nuns were bound by their aspiration to find loneliness and seclusion, to pursue asceticism and find a way to God. And yet it proved to be not only possible but also desirable to combine these aspirations with the city. A productive tension emerged between the various shades of monasticism and the various forms of urbanism. In this Element, we will investigate this peculiar relationship and its underlying mechanisms.

This is, then, not a history of monasticism.[1] It is not a phenomenology of its various shades or an all-encompassing analysis. Whether there is really such a thing as a core, unified monasticism, or whether we should really speak of different monasticisms is disputed.[2] After all, solitary stylites in Syria bore little outward resemblance to the brothers in Monte Cassino, or the sisters in a monastery in southern Gaul. We posit, however, that a certain peculiar relationship to cities is a widespread aspect of all forms of ancient Christian monasticism.

This world of Christian monasticism stretched from the Atlantic Ocean to the Persian Gulf, and it influenced and was influenced by a region even broader, stretching as far as Aksum in Ethiopia and Chang'an in central China (see Figure 1). This was not exclusively a Roman world. Other cultures and other modes of political organisation played a crucial role between 300 and 700 from Ireland to Mesopotamia. We use the term 'Broad Mediterranean' – for this inland sea remained a central infrastructure of exchange at the core of this region. What did it mean to be a monk or a nun in this world? There are arguably two main characteristics of this calling: personal asceticism and an impetus to leave the human world behind to find spiritual perfection. Monks and nuns saw themselves as full-time salvation seekers, which coincided with an urge to move away from civic society. These were prevalent *attitudes*, traceable mainly in monastic texts, that did not always translate into prevalent *practices*. For example, the Pachomian rules brought communal living to the fore, their coenobitism deeply rooted in the

---

[1] For an introduction to the history of monasticism, see Vanderputten 2020, pp. 1–2.

[2] Beach and Cochelin 2020.

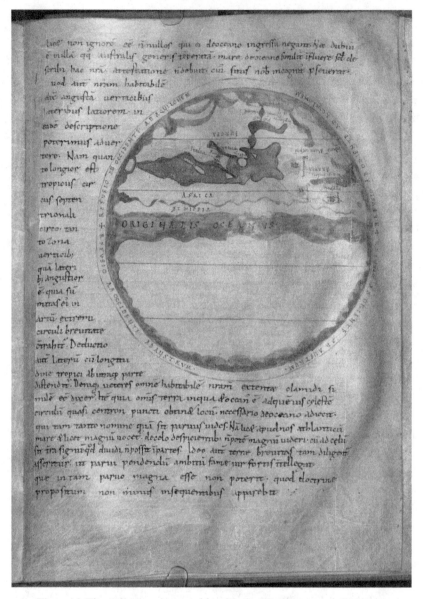

Figure 1 The Afroeurasian world, with the Mediterranean Sea at its centre. An eleventh-century map showing the world divided into climate zones. Bayerische Staatsbibliothek München, clm 6362, fol. 74r.
© Bayerische Staatsbibliothek München

urbanised world of Late Antiquity.[3] Pachomius' (c. 292–348) contemporary Anthony (c. 251–356) on the other hand was accepted from early on as the figurehead of eremitism. For him and his followers, seclusion and loneliness were paramount. These were not traits exclusive to Christian monasticism.[4] Similar attitudes and practices were common in Late Antiquity and the Early Middle Ages, such as wandering Cynics, Jewish ascetics, and Islamic mystics.[5] Opinions about who was or was not a monk or nun varied and these discussions were formative for the monastic movement. We should think of monasticism as a diverse, rhizomatic social movement, depending on a high degree of self-assertion and variable strategies of distinction. Already the earliest propagators of monasticism allowed for regional adaptability, frequently apart from institutionalising church structures.[6] As with many social movements, monasticism's inherent differences made it necessary to invest part of its energy 'in the effort to bind such differences together'.[7]

Monasticism was as diverse as cities. Thousands of pages have been devoted to defining urbanism and its various manifestations. From functionalist to categorist approaches, this forest makes us often miss the trees. No doubt it is necessary to consider individual and local circumstances – the bar is obviously different in fifth-century southern Gaul than it is in Egypt. The patterns of settlement differed greatly inside the Broad Mediterranean. In the East, many regions remained heavily urbanised, and cities even continued to expand in some cases. In the West, the scale of towns tended to be smaller, and the landscape overall less urbanised. The impact of economic and social changes was no doubt more visible in the West. 'The city' remained a diverse phenomenon when it came to size, economic standing, or prestige. Scholars today have to frame the late antique city not only through its physical appearance but first and foremost through the functions it fulfilled for its inhabitants.[8] As long as its observers and inhabitants saw it as something different, as long as it was capable of providing forms of surplus (not necessarily material), and as long as there was indication of marked internal organisation, we might call it a city.[9] In this frame, the city remained a focus of religious activity, elite representation, and political administration. This broad framework allows us to consider settlements ranging from classical

---

[3] Oexle 2011, p. 489.

[4] We concentrate on Christian monasticism. There were other non-Christian ascetic movements in this period as well. See Wimbush and Valantasis 2002.

[5] Livne-Kafri 1996.

[6] The church in our period was a collection of diverse structures and beliefs that were regionally specific. See Brown 2003, pp. 355–80.

[7] Melucci 1996, p. 13.   [8] Humphries 2019, p. 31.

[9] See Liebeschuetz 2001 and Grig 2013 for an overview of recent approaches.

civitates like Caesarea in Palestine to administrative capitals like Mainz, and to regional metropoleis like Alexandria.

Cities also had their own hinterlands that were functionally, ecclesiastically, and administratively connected to them. While the influence of a capital of a *pagus* might stretch for little more than a couple of kilometres, Constantinople had, arguably, a territory stretching thousands.[10] These *territoria* could intersect and mix, making some monasteries adjacent to more than one urban space. Monasteries and even individual monks often lived in what we will call 'spiritual suburbs': territories of urban settlements that were bound to them by religious concerns and routine interaction. These affiliations formed according to geographical proximity but also according to political, intellectual, and symbolic needs. The description of Oxyrhynchus in *Historia Monachorum in Aegypto* highlights thousands of monastics within the city walls and then even more in its territory. The text recognises the division between the city proper and 'the outer city [that] forms another town alongside the inner', made up from monasteries in its spiritual suburbs.[11] In some areas this concept was almost formalised. Sabas (439–532) was ordained the archimandrite of all the monasteries of the province of Palaestina Prima in 494. Even if the capital of the province was technically Caesarea, Sabas became in effect the superior of all the monasteries in the spiritual suburb of Jerusalem. In others, especially in the West, it remained less defined. Indeed, it is hard to find an expression of monasticism in Late Antiquity that did not find itself in a spiritual suburb of an urban space.[12] Even the only known stylite of the West, Wulfilaich (fl. c. 590), built his column in 'territorium Trevericae urbis'.[13]

Isidore of Seville (c. 560–636) in his *Etymologies* wrote: 'A city (*civitas*) is a multitude of people united by a bond of community . . . Now *urbs* (also "city") is the name for the actual buildings, while *civitas* is not the stone but the inhabitants'.[14] In the post-classical world a city was, from a perspective of a bishop and writer on monasticism, first and foremost a group of people living together. Therefore, in his mind, inhabitants of cities were not really that different from monks living in a monastery. Isidore writes: 'Cenobites whom we call those living "in a community", because a convent is of several people'.[15] We cannot go to Isidore for an analytical definition of a city. But we can read

---

[10] See Ward-Perkins 2000.

[11] *Historia Monachorum in Aegypto*, 5; see also Elm 1994, p. 329, f. 45.

[12] Peter Brown has seen Holy Men as living always close to settlements but more in the rural setting, and yet, as soon as they gathered followers, they would gravitate towards towns. They would also fulfill functions *of a town* for the villagers, like for example, litigation, see Brown 1971, pp. 84–5.

[13] Gregory of Tours, *Histories*, VIII, 15.   [14] Isidore, *Etymologiae*, XV.ii.1.

[15] Isidore, *Etymologiae*, VII.xiii.2.

him to understand what it felt like to live in one in Late Antiquity – it was as much a way of life as it was a group of buildings.

No city remained the same for the 400 years that this Element covers. Cities were transformed and were adapted to new circumstances. The uses of public spaces changed, the role of the church in cities' internal organisation increased, focal points of cities shifted, and authorities evolved new expectations of what cities were supposed to do. All the adaptations and transformations had effects on monasticism. Not only the city influenced monasticism, but the movement influenced the city as well. For 'cities are not simply material or lived spaces – they are also spaces of the imagination and spaces of representation. How cities are envisioned has effects'.[16]

Cities and monasteries found themselves in a field of tension. Changes to one side had reverberations on the other. To grasp these reverberations, we need to engage with a variety of sources with different outlooks on the problem. Aspects of this field of tension come out only in comparison. Therefore, this Element is built on a varied set of sources. It ranges from hagiographies and monastic rules through synodal acts and historiographies to archaeological excavations. They cover Greek, Latin, Syriac, Ge'ez, and Chinese texts from Ireland to China. Our hypothesis is that in all these sources we see the productive tension of monasticism and the city.

We invite the readers to come with us on an interpretative journey to trace how monasticism is illuminated by its persistent links to the city and how the late antique city was transformed by monasticism. We start by presenting a key metaphor – that of monasticism as a *genre* of society. In Section 2, we see how urban institutions influenced the conventions of monasticism. Late antique urban societies and the monks and nuns accommodated each other; from their arrangement the monastic *cives* was born. In Section 3, we look at monks and nuns *in* cities. Monastic writers and trendsetters figured out the correct distance to the busy markets and streets and came to terms with monastic presence on those very streets and markets. Monks and nuns were also a political force to be reckoned with, strategically adapting between life in the city and the monastery. Section 4 illuminates how the life of a monk or a nun required a considerable amount of daily study. Feeling that cities failed to deliver on the front of education, individual monks, nuns, and monasteries took matters into their own hands. This was a crucial step in their quest for a different, if not better, city. Section 5 takes us beyond Late Antiquity and the world of the Mediterranean shores. How can this urban-monastic framework help us understand what was going on in Sasanian Persia, Tang China, or the Islamic

---

[16] Bridge and Watson 2000, p. 7.

Caliphate? What was left to do for monks and nuns in worlds without cities or with weak ones like Ireland or post-Roman Britain? We close with a discussion of whether the monastery can be read as a *translatio* of the late antique city.

1 Monasticism as a Genre of Society

The first day when he came to stay there, he found a small piece of wood that had been inscribed thus by the brother who had lived there before him: 'I, Moses son of Theodore, am here and bearing witness.' The brother set the piece of wood before his eyes every day and asked the one who wrote it as though he were present, 'Where are you now, oh man, that you say, "I am present and bearing witness"? What kind of world are you in at this time? And where is the hand that wrote this?'
Apophthegmata Patrum N. 519–520

Monasticism was not a monolith but rather a network of currents – a variety of strands that formed a tapestry woven sometimes tighter, sometimes looser. For all strands of monasticism, your *community* was as important as asceticism – even if this community was sometimes experienced by living apart.[17] Becoming a monastic meant becoming a member of a community, and this community was never apart from broader society. Just like genres are categories of literature, so was monasticism a category of late antique society. Much like in a genre, be it romance or science fiction, to participate in monasticism you had to respect certain conventions. You could push them, changing the movement in the process, but there was always a horizon of expectation that you had to keep in sight if you did not want to lose your fellow monks and nuns or your lay audience. Over time the rules of this monastic genre became more rigid and the interpretative elbow room smaller. This process had an important gender dimension: female monasticism remained a space of experimentation longer and to a greater extent than male.[18] As with a good sonnet, there is real artistry in operating within a set of literary rules. And, in the twist of textual fate, this progressive institutionalisation was also expressed as a text: the monastic rule. The history of monasticism could then be read as a history of women and men that operated within a societal genre.[19]

This notion seems to be contradicted by ascetics that do not busy themselves with literature of any form or kind. Monks and nuns were, sometimes, seemingly far away from the literary world. As if they were simply not interested in taking part in the wider movement. The story of Mary of Egypt is a case in point. Mary did not write anything. Her character in the *vita* by Sophronius (c. 560–638), patriarch of Jerusalem, initially appears ignorant of all conventions that

---

[17] Goehring 1996.   [18] Diem 2013.
[19] Explaining social reality through textuality and using literature as a metaphor for society has precedent. See Brown 1987.

Figure 2 Mary of Egypt, holding the three loaves of bread. From St Germain l'Auxerrois in Paris, sixteenth century. Photo © mbzt / Wikimedia Commons / CC BY-SA 4.0

would make monasticism. She lives in Alexandria in the fifth century and hers is the life of promiscuity. She joins a group of pilgrims to Jerusalem, not with the intention of seeking salvation, but for getting sexual pleasure from the other travellers. Salvation and asceticism find her nonetheless. It is on Golgotha where she finally repents. She buys three loaves of bread and leaves for the desert (see Figure 2). For forty-seven years she does not encounter a single living soul. Finally, a monk named Zosimos finds her and listens to her story. Mary dies soon after, leaving a note in the sand, and Zosimos goes on to tell her tale. Her apparent obliviousness to literature, monasticism, or community did not hinder her story from becoming one of the staples of early medieval asceticism. Quite the contrary, from initial short remarks about a female ascetic by earlier authors, her story grew and evolved into the version that Sophronius so successfully put to parchment.[20] Mary did not intend to become part of the community and it would change nothing if she never existed in the first place. But she was taken in through progressive re-workings of her story, adapting her deeds into what was expected from an ascetic character. She became a staple of monasticism – her *vita* reached all regions and languages of the Broad Mediterranean, including Old English, Latin, and Syriac. This process of being taken into the genre is one key function of what we call literarisation.[21] The other function of this concept is exemplified by Jerome.

Jerome (c. 347–420), church father, translator of the Bible and prolific author, came from a wealthy family and had lived in Rome, Trier, and Aquileia. After years of studies and life as a young urban professional, he left everything behind to be alone, to fast, and do penance. He peddled a vision of that experience in his letters as eremitic and desert-like, characterised by isolation, in complete opposition to the pleasures of Rome. Jerome uses his connections and status to become a member of the monastic community: he spreads the story of his own ascetic experience. 'In the corner of the desert which stretches between the Syrians and the Saracens',[22] his monastic pedigree could take shape. Jerome takes his monastic credentials into his own hands. In Chalcis, he boasted having scribes at his disposal and a library.[23] He received correspondence and supplies, took language lessons, and annoyed local monks and clergy.[24] He also kept a watchful eye on the episcopal affairs in nearby Antioch.[25] Jerome desired to stay relevant and persuasive to others, like other prominent monks. Isolation and contemplation lent authority and lineage but their positive effects on any career were squandered when they led to irreversible social isolation.

This is also why 'going into the desert' was for Jerome a reversible act. Jerome stayed some three years in Chalcis, but he never lost touch with church politics and left the desert to get involved in those politics in Antioch and Constantinople. Whether he intended to make the desert his final home is difficult to say. The retreat to the desert was a never completed process or a singular act. The *monastic* desert was not fully attainable – one could only work towards it. It remained a pillar of monastic thought nonetheless.[26] As the

---

[20]　Sophronius of Jerusalem, *Life of Mary*.　　[21]　See Fafinski and Riemenschneider 2022.

[22]　Jerome, *Letters,* Ep. 7; a line that he repeats often, see Ep. 5.

[23]　Jerome, *Letters,* Ep. 22.7, 5.　　[24]　See Rebenich 2002.

[25]　Schlange-Schöningen 2018, p. 81.

[26]　Rapp 2006. See Eucherius, bishop of Lyon in the fifth century, and his *In Praise of the Desert*.

example of the Coptic *Life of Onnophrius* shows, desert asceticism consists of stages – and you could always go even deeper into the desert.[27] In this, the *Life of Anthony* might well have served as an example. The desert was not the ideal destination but the ideal direction: it was literarised at the hands of such authors like Jerome. While it might express a real experience, it ultimately expressed an ideology.[28]

To be a monk meant to engage with texts, be it through writing, interpretation, or enacting in practice. Literarisation allows you to become a member of a social movement either through getting written into the genre, writing yourself into it, or acting along its rules. All monastic literature is at least to a certain degree prescriptive.[29] Therefore, a concern with books, letters, and rules can signal who is in and who is out on monasticism.[30] This also meant an incentive to participate in a monastic history – an attempt to coordinate various strands of the monastic past. Monastic rules even prescribed writing down 'every deed and every word that occurs in their domain'.[31] The multivocality of monastic rules alone in Late Antiquity was immense.[32] The movement consequently had a semblance of coherence only as a set of texts in dialogue and in contradiction with each other.[33]

While ambitious authors and monastic activists like Jerome could use this to their advantage, it was not solely used by career-oriented elites. If we look at the anonymous *Historia Monachorum in Aegypto* (written around 400), we can see more modest pilgrims and monks deploying the image of the *eremos*, equally open to creative interpretations of what constituted loneliness and desert. The *Historia* is a fascinating report of a group of seven monks who visited the most renowned eremites of Egypt. The travelling monks were likely members of the monastery on the Mount of Olives founded by Jerome's close acquaintance and 'frenemy' Rufinus (345–411). These monks were keen on gathering the wisdom of the desert fathers, but they were also fascinated by the desert experience. In the prologue, the author exclaims that 'they [the Egyptian eremites] do not busy themselves with any earthly matter' but 'live as true citizens of heaven'. Some, the author says, 'do not even know that another world exists on earth, or that evil is found in cities'. Instead, they dwell 'scattered in the desert waiting for Christ'.[34] Therefore, it seems strange that the account of their first encounter with another monk – John, said to be a clairvoyant – describes anything but a secluded hermit, waiting for Christ. John used his gift to predict the tide of the

---

[27] *Life of Onnophrius*.   [28] Goehring 2003, pp. 441–2.
[29] See Jonas of Bobbio, *Life of Columbanus*.   [30] See Williams 2006.
[31] Shenoute, *Rules*, n. 474.   [32] Diem and Rousseau 2020.
[33] A fact that late antique authors were consciously engaging, see Westergren 2018.
[34] *Historia Monachorum in Aegypto*, prologue 6–7.

Nile, the victory of emperor Theodosius, an incursion of wild nomads, and the death of the same emperor. The author even admits that John was a minor celebrity in the region. He received clients and helped them with various issues. The first two clients are a tribune and a *praepositus*, both having marriage troubles. Despite all these earthly concerns, the author insists that John was an example of someone who had 'renounced the world fully and completely'. Here we see how the rules of the genre were pushed but not broken.

John is not an isolated example. Monks living in the desert (or its local equivalent) remain involved in urban and secular life. We see how closely the monastic spiritual suburb was integrated with city life in the collection of letters by Barsanuphius and (another) John, two sixth-century spiritual 'advice columnists'.[35] They know what is going on in Gaza and the surrounding cities. They know the prices of various services and goods on the local markets; they are asked to arbitrate on matters concerning the election of the city's bishop; they advise city magistrates on their complaints to the emperor. Both seem keenly aware of the trappings of city life, be it judicial proceedings, the use of baths, or seeking medical advice. At the same time, their engagement against theatrical performances betrays their concerns about what is happening in the city (and intimate knowledge of the circus and the laws surrounding it). Barsanuphius and John are exceptional in the number of letters (over 800) that have survived but not in their activities or knowledge. They are a testimony to the integration of the withdrawn monks in the workings of urban bureaucracy and daily life.[36] Their membership of the community is in no way endangered by this literary activity. They engage in classical literary tropes and advise passing books (presumably including pagan authors) to a monastery.[37] While their letters concern mainly other monks, they are also inhabited by magistrates, advocates, city bishops, and shopkeepers – and perhaps even more in letters not preserved by later editors and compilers for whom the *minutiae* of late antique city may have lost comprehensibility and usefulness as time passed. Here, two monks answer to a vital need of ascetics in Late Antiquity: they respond to everyday concerns of those unsure if they follow the rules of the genre correctly. They also exhibit how having these questions and providing those answers was intertwined with city life.

Monasticism as a genre is an apt metaphor for the range of social phenomena we will encounter on the following pages. There are shades, there are differences, and there are common themes. We propose that literarisation regulates

---

[35] On their letter collection see Hevelone-Harper 2016.
[36] Barsanuphius and John, *Letters*, Letters 627, 802, 831, 449, 771, 508, 770, 836, 837; see also Weiss 2014, p. 231.
[37] Barsanuphius and John, *Letters*, Letters 131, 453, 493, 137b, 326.

the rules and conventions of this genre. Written texts and social reality intersect in a way that we can observe. One influences the other and we will never be able to reconstruct the social reality of monasticism without acknowledging this fact. Monastic literature is not intelligible without the existence, the reality, of hermitages and monasteries. Monastic texts, worlds, and archaeologies converge in our picture of this crucial movement of Late Antiquity and the Early Middle Ages.

2 The Monastery as a City

We also went to Oxyrhynchus, one of the cities of the Thebaid. It is impossible to do justice to the marvels which we saw there. For the city is so full of monasteries that the very walls resound with the voices of monks. Other monasteries encircle it outside, so that the outer city forms another town alongside the inner. The temples and capitols of the city were bursting with monks; every quarter of the city was inhabited by them.

Historia Monachorum in Aegypto, V

This description of the Egyptian city of Oxyrhynchos from the early fifth century paints a striking picture. The *Historia Monachorum* was not a niche text – it was one of the most widely read monastic writings of Late Antiquity and the Early Middle Ages, regularly on the parchment bestseller lists, not least thanks to its Latin version composed by Rufinus.[38] It influenced the image of Egyptian monasticism in the eyes of thousands of monks, nuns, and laypeople from York to Persia. It is also wishful thinking.

Oxyrhynchos did not have '10 000 monks and 20 000 nuns', as one of the seven monks from the monastery at Mount of Olives who penned this account would like the readers to believe. But that fact was largely irrelevant. What *was* relevant is that already at the turn of the fourth and fifth centuries, monasticism and monks were seen as fitting into an image of a provincial, Roman city in Egypt; that such a description would be seen as not only believable but also useful for the cause; and that there were more women than men among the monastics. Monks and monasteries could appear anywhere; despite the legacy of desert dwellers, monasticism profited from its urban links. Most importantly, one could imagine a city essentially living its urban life as a monastery. The lay inhabitants in Oxyrhynchos played a second fiddle. In this literary representation, the city *is* a monastery, an urban machine geared towards seeking salvation, where all the secular functions aim at serving the monks and nuns. The Greek version of the *Historia* claimed that there were 'almost more monks than lay people'[39] in the city – the balance had tipped.

---

[38] See Cain 2016, pp. 1–8; 2019, pp. 12–20.   [39] *Historia Monachorum in Aegypto*, ch. 5.

How did a movement so strongly based on withdrawal start to uphold the urban landscape? One of the key reasons was how quickly monasteries, whether located in a rural or an urban context, began to resemble Roman cities in many of their characteristics and functions. The monastic formation was also strongly influenced by the civic discourse.[40]

In the eyes of city dwellers and clerics alike, monasteries and cities resembled each other. 'You are a guest in your own [urban] *domus*, so that you become a dweller of Paradise and a citizen of your true native city',[41] wrote Paulinus of Nola (c. 345–431) to his friend Severus upon hearing of his entry into a monastery. 'You have received a kind of a city of your own, pious citizens', wrote Cassiodorus (c. 490–585) to his community.[42] Being a monk was about being a citizen of a more perfected city.[43] To understand how this convergence of functions that ultimately led to urban skeuomorphism of many monasteries came to pass, we need to start with two extraordinary women.

Monastic Euergetism

Roman elites traditionally were patrons of cities, through various forms of legal protection and in financial investment in buildings, statues, and infrastructure. Whole families could tie themselves to particular cities. Civic euergetism, the practice of investing private money in public space to gain prestige, was a pinnacle of the urban face of the Roman Empire.[44] This activity was not limited to men, but female patrons were significantly less frequent.[45]

Patronage was not only about status but also about economic stability, career opportunities, and building a political base. Cities could only offer those benefits if they remained stable and were seen as a place of opportunity. Urban patronage remained a calculation of economic and symbolic values. The arrival of Christianity did not upend this paradigm – if anything, it offered new avenues and possibilities.[46] But soon a new actor appeared that offered a parallel option, both rooted in the city and present in the rural landscape: the monastery.

In the lives of the two Melanias – the Elder (c. 350–410) and the Younger (c. 383–439) – we see how an aristocratic family through three and possibly four generations could use monasticism as an alternative for what urbanism had offered. Both Melanias were among the richest women in Roman history who became important figures in the Roman Empire and the Christian church. They were also active patronesses of monasteries and monasticism in general. Their

---

[40] Westergren 2018.　　[41] Paulinus of Nola, *Letters*, 11.4.
[42] Cassiodorus, *Institutions*, 1.32.3.　　[43] Rapp 2019.　　[44] Veyne 1976; Salzman 2017.
[45] Hemelrijk 2004.　　[46] Wood 2018.

commitment is probably the best example of how Roman aristocrats could continue to fulfil their roles as benefactors and maintain their status – yet in a new, monastic, reality.[47] Crucially, most of our information concerning the two comes from monastic sources – the *Vita Melaniae* by Gerontius, and Palladius' *Historia Lausiaca*, both from the early fifth century.

What did they do? The Melanias frequented cities but also stayed formally on top of their families and fortunes. They continued to pull profit from the vast agricultural enterprise that had sustained the family for centuries but chose to stabilise their social positions by investing in monastic communities. Both Melanias appear to have been pious Christian women and monasteries provided them with a form of prestige that supplanted the effects of civic euergetism. The returns on their investments appear to have been considerable: the status and wealth of the younger Melania was in no way diminished by the course of action of her grandmother. Her own choice of spending all the money and not retaining a family fortune did stop the traditional view of aristocratic continuity,[48] but it did not make her any less of a central figure of the empire.

Melania the Elder's involvement in monasticism allowed for multiple opportunities. The foundation of a brotherhood on the Mount of Olives enabled the patronage of a prolific Christian writer, Rufinus of Aquileia. At the same time, neither of the two women lost their connection with urban spaces, both intellectually and practically. Their pedigree as Christian benefactresses led them to travel frequently to Rome, Jerusalem, or Constantinople. Melania the Younger still managed to visit Constantinople shortly before her death to convert her uncle Volusianus, an important official at the imperial court.[49] We should not discount the piety behind that move. But we can also not ignore the importance of this conversion for cementing their family's monastic empire. The fact that Augustine (354–430) had chastised Melania the Younger for continually giving her monasteries cash and not estates, speaks volumes both about the prominence of Melania, and about her active role in the management of her fortune.[50] This was also a Broad Mediterranean enterprise: the family estates stretched from Britain to Africa. A massive fire sale of many of these estates was initiated in 408 due to the political crisis in Italy and the desire for greater asceticism. Endangered estates were converted into ready cash that went almost immediately into supporting monastic foundations.[51] As a result, Melania's influence

---

[47] On the Melanias, see Cooper 2005; Chin and Schroeder 2016; Clark 2020.

[48] In fact the longevity of aristocratic families in Rome (and therefore their dynastic stability) was not particularly long, see Scheidel 1999.

[49] Gerontius, *Life of Melania*, 55.

[50] Gerontius, *Life of Melania*, 20; on Augustine's stance on wealth and power see Brown 2005.

[51] Brown 2013, pp. 297–9.

only increased, and assets were withdrawn from regions immediately threatened by crisis like Britain or Italy. There is a potent metaphor in scions of the richest Roman families investing hundreds of thousands of solidi into monasteries, on the eve of Alaric's three-day-long organised divestment of urban riches in Rome. The actual rules of how this patronage should look were forged on the fly.[52] Overall, the family of both Melanias had a consistent strategy for a period of over sixty years – a strategy that was based on monastic euergetism.[53] Its success was possible not because monasteries were an opposite to the city but because they were so alike.

The Christian monastic matrix awarded the Melanias a kind of freedom and prestige that were otherwise unattainable to them as women. For them, the monastery was the *better* city. Female patronage of monasticism became an opportunity not to be missed, seized by other important women as well.[54] Paula (347–404) – the benefactress of Jerome and contemporary of Melania the Elder – had built Jerome a city in miniature. To further the stature of her protégé and the value of her investment, she furnished his monastery with its own library, school, scriptorium, and even defensive walls. This was a 'city' over which she exerted unprecedented influence. She also founded a similar establishment for herself and her nuns.[55]

In fact, noble women stood on the forefront of a development that made monasteries the pillars of elite sustainability.[56] They extracted symbolic and actual capital from the city, while never leaving the city behind. Marcella's *suburbanus ager* where she lived with her friends was only rhetorically outside of the city: in fact, it was right on the Aventine and served as a lynchpin of elite connections.[57] This new strategy and behaviour found ready reception in broad circles of the aristocracy in the Latin West as well. The initial – and sporadically recurring – resistance to it highlights how monasteries supplemented cities as anchors of influence. The reality in southern Gaul was not that different: John Cassian (c. 360–435) was a stark defendant of sincere asceticism and seclusion in the first decades of the fifth century, and one of the most recognised propagators of monasticism in the West.[58] As one would expect, he loudly praised efforts to make Gallic monks follow the ideal of anchoretic life and leave the city.[59] Yet, Cassian was part of a network of noblemen, abbots, bishops, and prolific Christian authors. This network was reliant on urban infrastructure and monastic foundations. John himself, building on the patronage of his peers,

---

[52] Cooper 2007a.   [53] Chin and Schroeder 2016.   [54] Cooper 2005.
[55] Brown 2013, p. 279.
[56] See Brown 2015 for the spiritual underpinning of this development.
[57] Letsch-Brunner 1998.   [58] Rousseau 1978.
[59] John Cassian, *The Conferences*, b211–b212.

founded two monasteries in the city of Marseille.[60] Even if monastic patronage was on the rise, and money going away from civic infrastructure, the city was here to stay.

This form of patronage would go on in the post-Roman period. Gregory of Tours' (c. 538–594) account of the life of Gallus (c. 489–553), a first-born son of a senatorial family from Clermont-Ferrand, is a vivid example.[61] When young Gallus decided to go to the monastery, his father, although he wanted him to marry, was more than happy for this to happen. While we read here the thoughts of Gregory, who was inclined to portray monastic life as an uncontroversial choice, we cannot help to wonder why that was. To mention the worry of the father yet have him give in to his son's vocation made perfect sense when you wanted to further Christian asceticism. There is a second layer to the story, though. The monastery of Cournon, where Gallus eventually became a monk, lay in the spiritual suburbs of Clermont, barely 10 kilometers from the city's centre and offered an attractive investment into his son's future. Cournon presented fabulous prospects for ambitious and well-to-do regional noblemen. One could become abbot but there was more on the line: if everything went well, there was also the possibility of the bishop's see. Apart from education, spiritual perfection, and a network of influential churchmen, Cournon was a viable route to high office that could sustain a noble family. For Gallus these hopes were fulfilled: he did not take his eyes off the prize and became the bishop of his city, Clermont. This was the expected outcome: money and status were as easily transferable to an ecclesiastical (and monastic) career as they were useful for an old-fashioned civic one. A new model of *domus* management was being forged.[62] Did it work in the long run? Apparently yes: after all, Gallus was Gregory's uncle.[63]

Here we need to remind ourselves that monasticism and its traditions were heavily literarised. The story of Gallus is more telling if we read it as an example of the idealised harmony between secular elites and the world of the church. Yet if Gregory describes the interaction between the elite and Cournon in such detail, it was relatable to his audience. The willing father of Gallus is then not only a stand-in for a pious aristocrat. He is also a signal for Gregory's audience that the civic and urban solutions were not contradictory to monasticism, nor was the aristocratic way of life.[64] Building and sponsoring monasteries was propagated as both furthering your standing and shortening your way into ecclesiastical office by the end of the sixth century.

---

[60] See Goodrich 2007. [61] Gregory of Tours, *Lives and Miracles*, ch. 6.
[62] Cooper 2007b, p. 235. [63] For a more cautious view see Wood 2022, pp. 25–6.
[64] For a different view of the Gallus case see Jones 2009, p. 95.

The proof for this hypothesis comes to us in the form of a lamentation. Pope Gregory the Great (c. 540–604) complained to Gallic bishops how building monasteries was misused as a way of atoning for simony and facilitating getting into office, a practice he deemed illegal.[65] He was terrified that such a pragmatic approach to holy institutions might spread in the West.[66] In the East, the bishop of Neapolis on Cyprus, Leontius, attests to the normalisation of noble patronage. He saw the building of monasteries as part of the regular public service, on par with endowing almshouses and houses for the old.[67] These were framed as services to the poor in the city, once more highlighting that monasteries had become part of the urban landscape, even if they were often situated in its outskirts. Patronage of monasteries thus became the bread and butter of the late antique Christian rich and powerful.

From the end of the fourth century, many facets of monasticism were not only bound to cities but also began to offer attractive and viable symbolic investment opportunities. They offered income, career options for multiple members of the family (including, for more or less the first time, women who could become abbesses), and the possibility of monastic euergetism. For ambitious and rich aristocratic families, monasteries could be stand-ins for cities. This is true for the intellectual level as well: patronising monasteries gave those families close access to important literary and spiritual circles of the day.

In the late sixth- and early seventh-century West, monasteries might have overtaken most of the practical urban functions. We observe a progressive institutionalisation as monasteries supplanted civic euergetism, offered educational possibilities for the elite and an alternative or continuation of a secular career. They also increasingly played a role in other areas traditionally connected with the urban space like health care.[68] This unique position of being *like* a city soon started to influence another area of life: economy.

Economy and Law

Sometime in the fifth century, somewhere in Palestine, perhaps in the Great Laura of St Sabas, a monk named Gelasius lost his book (see Figure 3). It was not an ordinary book – it was a parchment codex of the Bible 'containing both the Old and the New Testament' worth eighteen solidi. One solidus could buy you enough bread for a year.[69] The book lay in the church of the monastery for

[65] Gregory the Great, *Letters*, 9.219.

[66] Parallels were made with this practice and the classical praxis of sponsoring a public building in order to make yourself eligible for public office. See Goddard 2021.

[67] Leontios of Neapolis, *Life of St John the Almsgiver*.   [68] Crislip 2005.   [69] Jones 1965, p. 8.

Figure 3 The monastery of St Sabas in the Judean desert. Photo: Mateusz Fafinski

all brothers to read (which means they were able to read it or were at least expected to). But a monk visiting the monastery stole it to sell it. What follows is a slapstick story of back-and-forth visits and negotiations framed as an educational tale about monastic property and the virtue of poverty. More important for us is the fact that the monk-thief went straight to the city with his booty where he sought out a bookseller to fence the goods. The bookseller was unsure of the price, so he needed someone to evaluate the book; and who better than...

Gelasius to do this job! At the end, the monk-thief ends up giving the book back and staying at the monastery of Gelasius.[70]

This anecdote from the *Apophthegmata Patrum* is telling. Monks in this episode are bound economically to the city – and not just through the purchase and sale of simple wares but through a rather specialised activity like booksell-ing. Gelasius ends up being an appraiser for the urban bookseller, who goes to the monk without a particular divine intervention. The anonymous author of the episode is well informed about the prices and particularities of urban trade. The economic connections between the city and the monastery were rich, diverse, and completely normal. They were not problematic in a text that would be the spiritual bedrock for many late ancient monks.[71]

In the late antique context, especially in regions like Palestine, Egypt, or southern Gaul, monasteries had to be included within the existing economic networks and those centred on cities. Papyri evidence confirms that for Egypt Pachomian-style communities (*koinobia*) were socially and economically inte-grated in their neighbouring villages and towns.[72] The oldest Gallic rules also mention how brothers are supposed to prepare themselves for business on the outside. Monasteries from the onset were not separate from the urban econ-omies, just as the individual monks themselves were tied to their secular communities.[73] Augustine's rule provided for business to be done in the city, specifically referencing the sale of monastic products.[74] There is an early understanding that monastic establishments had a symbiotic relationship with the city.

This put monasteries in a seemingly complicated situation. While anticipated to be places of retreat they in fact quickly became integrated in the urban economy. In Egypt, they started to administer estates and became hubs of pilgrim related economy, which influenced even the form of their buildings.[75] Economic necessities soon shifted the spiritual conventions of the social genre of Egyptian monasticism.

If we go back to the *Historia Monachorum*, in the life of abba Sarapion (fl. 4th c.), we encounter a glimpse of this process. Apart from giving spiritual guidance, Sarapion took on the role of an estate administrator. His monks were working in the fields, both those of their monastery and of neighbouring properties. He himself oversaw their activities and kept the accounts and organised regular shipments of produce – mostly grain and ready-made

---

[70] *Apophthegmata Patrum*, p. 289.

[71] Over centuries, the *Apophthegmata* were used, re-worked, translated and copied: Rubenson 2013.

[72] Goehring 1993.   [73] Tutty 2017.   [74] *Rule of Augustine,* Ordo monasterii, VIII.

[75] Goehring 1999, pp. 39–52; Blanke 2020.

clothing – to Alexandria.[76] Already at the end of the fourth century, economic achievements were a laudable thing for monks. At the same time, the monastic economy needed cities as market outlets. Even the *Regula Benedicti* stipulates that goods from the monastery were to be sold – if slightly beneath the market price.[77]

In the sixth century, a monastery in Palestine housing twenty monks was expected to produce a sizeable surplus. The monastery at Khirbet es-Suyyagh was founded on the site of an earlier agricultural productive site.[78] It lay in a triangle between the cities of Nicopolis (Emmaus), Eleutheropolis, and Jerusalem. The monastery welcomed pilgrims and was equipped with a church, storage units, and an impressive outer wall with a tower. Its most important economic features were several oil and wine presses. The presses were used as a communal facility for peasants in the area, yet the monks also had olive groves and vineyards of their own. Used to capacity, the presses allowed for an annual surplus of many thousand litres of both wine and oil.[79] Additionally, the monastery owned a small quarry and pastured animals. It sold its surplus in cities. We know nothing about this monastery from written sources but given the archaeology, it is fair to say that the abbot was in a similar position as abba Sarapion. He was (also) a manager of an agricultural enterprise that was intertwined not only with its surrounding peasant communities but also with the surrounding cities. Monasteries became a crucial link in the economic chain, processing local produce and passing it on to urban markets.

Now, the question is why monasteries became productive bodies so soon. As our discussion of monastic euergetism and sponsorship suggests, this could have had to do with secular donors who wanted to draw all kinds of profit from their investments. Another important factor was the motivation to help the poor and act as stabilisers for communities. This presupposes a strong link to secular society that monastic rhetoric often denied. But when we look closely, the sources show strong hints that many monks, nuns, and monasteries cared a lot, and that active concern was one of their main traits. Nothing shows this better than a short letter from our dear friend Barsanuphius. Upon being asked by someone whether it was important to 'keep the accounts of the church', Barsanuphius responded:

> If you keep the accounts of a church, you are actually keeping the accounts of God. For you are God's steward. Therefore, you are obliged to keep the accounts in such a way as to feed the poor and the orphans, should there be any surplus. After all, God is their Father and nurturer, and you are

---

[76] *Historia Monachorum in Aegypto*, nr. 18.   [77] *The Rule of Benedict*, ch. 57.

[78] As were most of the monasteries of this period and region, Taxel 2009, p. 219.

[79] Taxel 2009, pp. 211–12.

administering their goods. If there is no surplus, you should do whatever you
can to produce one. Otherwise, you are not keeping the accounts of a church
but only intending to take care of yourself.[80]

We do not know the position of the person who is asking about the 'accounts of the
church', but they did ask a monk for advice. Barsanuphius was a hermit in the hills
of Gaza, connected to the larger monastery of Seridos. His honest opinion: if you
were busy with producing anything, you should be a scrupulous bookkeeper, and
you should of course make a profit. It would be sinful not to do so. As a faithful
Christian, your task was to take care of yourself and your surroundings and you
could only do that if you were turning a profit as it could be used charitably.

This openness towards the different roles a monk could take on was by no
means restricted to the eastern Mediterranean. John Cassian was one of the first
monastic authors to propagate a multivocal vision of being a monk. Following the
example of St Anthony was but one way to achieve humility and perfection.
Monks with different talents could choose different paths as well: offering
hospitality, educating and guiding their brothers, or treating the ill and the poor.
All those were valid fields of engagement that did not stand in conflict with strict
eremitism.[81] All of these activities required access to money and people.

It made perfect sense to treat monasteries as economic entities bound to both
rural communities and cities. The fact that large medieval monasteries like Fulda,
Cluny, or Murbach would turn out to hold large and productive properties is, then,
partly the consequence of this early development. Despite their established
rhetoric, monasteries would want to be involved in secular society, and want to
emulate the possibilities of cities. A grand showing of their economic prowess,
like the famous bronze doors of Monte Cassino from the early twelfth century,
depicting all its estates and meant to prove its wealth, should be read
accordingly[82] – not as a deviation from the true form, but as an expression of
the capabilities of monasticism. Moreover, these monasteries were functioning *as*
cities, as focal point of their own *territorium*, with their own agricultural hinterland. Be it the monks of Sarapion, the peasants near Khirbet es-Suyyagh, or the
estates of Monte Cassino, they were all organised around a monastery. If it were
not for those monasteries, agricultural production would need another point of
distribution and processing. This also differentiates monasteries from villas, even
though they retained elements of this form of economic organisation as well.[83]
Monasteries were axes of communities, market outlets, brokers, and centres of
population – they were analogous to small towns.

---

[80] Barsanuphius and John, *Letters*, 828.   [81] John Cassian, *The Conferences*, 14.4.
[82] Bloch 1987.
[83] On the process of conversion of villas to monasteries in Gaul, see Percival 1997.

Assuming social roles usually considered to be urban also had a legal aspect. The coenobitic form of monasticism was quickly and radically treated like cities in the legal world of the imperial bureaucracy. The first legislation about monasteries and monks is not ecclesiastical but secular. In the 370s, Valens legislated against 'devotees of idleness' deserting their service in municipalities and joining 'bands of hermit monks'.[84] The first laws dealing with monks have to do with the city: the laws first prohibiting and then allowing monks to live in the city are an early example of the secular legislators trying to come to terms with the new movement.[85] They tell us that monks started to be a frequent sight on the city streets and that the position of secular authority vis-à-vis this phenomenon was still being negotiated.

This was happening long before the Council of Chalcedon delivered a preliminary position of the church on monasteries and monks in 451. We should not view the inactivity of the institutionalised church as indifference.[86] The leaders of the church were very much interested in monasticism; yet they seem to have expressed their concern first and foremost to the imperial bureaucracy. The Theodosian law limiting free movement of monks appears as a product of heavy lobbying by those in the imperial entourage keen on exerting their considerable influence on the development of monasticism.[87] They did not, however, try to achieve their goals through ecclesiastical legislation. Even the canons of Chalcedon concerning monasticism are mainly due to local imperial and urban influence and not internal considerations of the church. When it comes to law, monks until the sixth century appear mostly in societal and not in spiritual contexts. Indeed, Justinian still felt it was necessary to legislate against monks wandering the city streets at night and frequenting taverns.[88]

Monks appear in legislation either as dwellers of cities or of town-like corporations, that is, monasteries. Monasteries had by the end of the fifth century started adopting the same legal procedure vis-à-vis secular authority as cities.[89] It has been observed that monasteries could act as *collegia* giving them privileges of corporate bodies both in law and in acquiring wealth.[90] This system shows unprecedented stability in both East and West, surviving way into the Middle Ages and beyond. The durability of this arrangement has to do with corporations, legal fictions, and the activities of the monks themselves.

In antiquity, cities could petition the emperor for a rescript – as such they possessed the ability to act as a corporative legal entity to ask for a resolve of a dispute or to obtain privileges, exemptions, or immunities for their

---

[84] *Codex Theodosianus*, 12.1.63.   [85] *Codex Theodosianus*, 16.3.1–2.   [86] Isola 2006.
[87] Wipszycka 2018.   [88] *Corpus Iuris Civilis*, Novel 133.   [89] Wojtczak 2019.
[90] See Wood 2006, pp. 729–39; Wood 2022, p. 102.

inhabitants. Perhaps the most celebrated case of such activity is the petition and the subsequent corruption scandal involving Leptis Magna and emperor Valentinian.[91] In the legal landscape of Christianity's growing independence, the importance of monasteries helped them achieve almost similar ability: either acting on their own or through their founders or benefactors.

There is a telling analogy to pinpoint the similarity of monasteries and cities in this context. Synesius of Cyrene was, among other things, a nobleman in northern Africa around the year 400. While he would later serve as bishop of the whole province, he was sent to Constantinople in 398 as a representative of his hometown's secular elite. His goal was, predictably, to petition the emperor to grant certain tax exemptions to Cyrene (and probably the province as well). He would then stay in Constantinople for several years engaging in court politics.[92] Fast forward a hundred years, and here we have Sabas (439–532) going to Constantinople to petition for a tax relief for monasteries in the Judean desert and for the whole diocese of Jerusalem in 511 and 530. He would also stay for a longer time, lobbying the most important women of the court of Anastasius over the winter. Just as Synesius seems to have been part of a group of representatives, so was Sabas originally only one of several monks and abbots that were sent to Constantinople by the bishop of Jerusalem. These missions were providing for a new legal footing of monasteries. Not only did Sabas take a mediatory role that had been reserved for lay provincial elites before but he also makes clear the factual legal equivalence of the city and the monastery. He even goes as far as to petition Justinian for military protection and is sent home with corresponding rescripts.[93]

Acting like a city or being treated like one by the law were all pathways available to monasteries. They were inhabiting a legal fiction of Roman law. But they were also legally integrated with the *territoria* of late antique cities. This plethora of arrangements is stunning. Geographically, monasteries found themselves in cities, at their outskirts, or at a considerable physical but not practical distance. This made flexible options necessary and led to interesting results.

The famously rich and influential monastery of Corbie acquired from the Merovingian kings exemptions in the Mediterranean haven of Fos. Fos had been used as the port of Arles in the late Roman period, and later seems to have been integrated into the *territorium* of Marseille. From the middle of the seventh century, Corbie (over 800 kilometres to the north) was allowed to import numerous goods including pepper, cinnamon, papyrus, leather, and rice through Fos. Corbie secured the rights to import those goods tax-free first from Childeric

---

[91] Ammianus, *History*, 28.6.   [92] See Tanaseanu-Döbler 2008, pp. 156–7.
[93] Cyril of Scythopolis, *Lives of the Monks of Palestine*, 54, 70, 74.

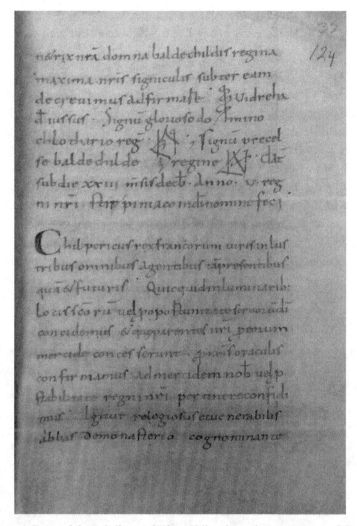

Figure 4 Copy of the privilege of King Chilperic to the monastery of Corbie, listing good as diverse as papyrus and cinnamon, preserved in a cartulary from the early tenth century. Staatsbibliothek zu Berlin Ms. Phill. 1776, fol. 124v

II and then again from Chilperic II in 716 (see Figure 4).[94] Apart from an almost representative example of acting like a city (asking and being granted tax exemptions), the story of Corbie's trade mission also shows how a monastery could be integrated into a *territorium* of a city – in this case Marseille – located many days travel away. It thus turned Corbie into a strangely familiar

[94] MGH DRF, n. 171; on the significance of the charter and the controversies about Chilperic II's confirmation, see McCormick 2001, p. 65.

phenomenon: a separate, spiritual suburb that was partly integrated into Marseille, partly an independent city-like legal and economic entity.

The Built Environment

Monasteries, with their patrons, their para-urban position in law and economy, and their corporately organised inhabitants also resembled cities in their built environment. Monasteries in the Judean desert were so densely placed that in most cases one did not need to walk longer than a couple of hours to stumble upon one. Since Derwas Chitty made those observations over fifty years ago, we have made significant steps towards better understanding both the internal structure of the monasteries and their relationship with cities.[95] Most monks needed less than a day to reach the city of Jerusalem and the monasteries were connected by a network of paths and roads.[96] Larger establishments, like the Martyrios monastery, resembled small towns. This was of course still nothing compared to the largest monasteries in Egypt. While even monasteries in remote locations like St Catherine in Sinai resembled small towns (see Figure 5), the famous White Monastery comprised an area of over seven hectares.[97]

Figure 5 St Catherine's monastery in the Sinai; it was almost a small town, with one of the most influential libraries. Photo: Mateusz Fafinski

---

[95] Chitty 1966.   [96] Hirschfeld 1992, p. 206.   [97] Blanke 2019, p. 119.

The situation in the West was no different, even if the scale was smaller. In places like southern Gaul there were multiple examples of the co-relationship of monasteries and cities. The monastery of Saint-André-le-Bas in Vienne was founded in 543 in the corner of the Roman walls of the city. Other monasteries that existed in the urban context, like the two foundations of John Cassian in Marseille, still await their discovery and archaeological survey.

Almost all urban-monastic phenomena remain mostly invisible for us archaeologically even if we know about their existence from the written sources. Small monastic communities existing in private town or suburban houses remain almost untraceable.[98] There are, of course, exceptions – like the *monasterium Boethianum* in Largo Argentina, right in the middle of late antique Rome (see Figure 6).[99] Or the monastic complex constructed by Augustine next to the cathedral of Hippo through merging a number of houses into what can be called a monastic half-insula.[100] Family-centred foundations are only detectable to us if they reached larger proportions. We might also miss them or question their identification because the monastery form is so compatible with that of the normal, garden-variety Roman *domus*.

Figure 6 The Monasterium Boethianum incorporated the structures of the Republican temple precinct, right in the middle of Rome. Photo: Mateusz Fafinski

---

Luxeuil, a foundation of Columbanus, an Irish monk in Gaul, is where rhetorical posturing meets reality in a visible way. Jonas of Bobbio, Columbanus' hagiographer, describes Luxeuil as a desert foundation, meant to provide a stark contrast with the inhabited environment. But the archaeological excavations from the beginning of the twenty-first century revealed a rich settlement and funerary landscape centred around a *castrum* of the former *vicus* of Luxovium, with a sizeable funerary basilica and a continuous use from the late Empire up to the Merovingian period. Jonas mentions that the baths and hot springs were still functional[101] and that the Irish community moved within a landscape of late Roman Christian settlement. Columbanus gets arrested *in atrium* of a church in Luxeuil, a feature absent from any Irish foundations but often found in late antique episcopal churches in Gaul.[102] For the standards of late sixth-century Merovingian Gaul this was at least a para-urban landscape.[103] In this respect, Luxeuil seems to be more like the monastery of St Maximin in Trier: founded in the sixth century around a late Roman funerary basilica directly outside the city walls.

In the East, there existed other, and quite different, para-urban monasteries. Kellia (literally: 'the Cells') was a large monastic complex west of the Nile delta at the entrance to the Libyan desert. It has been extensively excavated from the 1960s onwards, revealing a vast landscape of largely standardised hermitage dwellings that formed a joined organism housing upwards from 1,500 monks in the best of times.[104] The monks lived in small clusters, furnished with latrines, plumbing, and numerous communal spaces, with a church and commercial quarter as well as hostels for pilgrims and storage facilities. Those 'fora' where monks met and interacted with each other as well as with the visitors are reminiscent of Roman cities. This was a settlement of incredible stability, with generations of masons and builders expanding, rebuilding, and maintaining it between the fourth and the ninth centuries.[105] With time, Kellia attracted pilgrims and celebrity monks. For monks accustomed to the metropolitan world of Constantinople and Jerusalem it might have seemed to be a backwater in the desert.[106] But the built environment of Kellia reveals a settlement that truly was a monastic town.

The monastery of Hilarion near Gaza is another good example of this phenomenon. Hilarion is one of the famous (and notorious) examples of early monasticism. After his death, he was buried in the cave that he had chosen as his first solitary enclosure. Near Maiuma, the port of Gaza, a monastery was subsequently built and thrived in the sixth century. It lay close to the road from Egypt to Gaza

---

[101] Jonas of Bobbio, *Life of Columbanus*, 17.   [102] Bully et al. 2014, p. 354.
[103] Hammer 2012.   [104] Guillaumont et al. 1991.   [105] Brooks Hedstrom 2017, pp. 255–62.
[106] Palladius, *The Lausiac History*, 38.10.

and was a natural attraction for pilgrims on their way to the Holy Land. Apart from a mosaic with an inscription that sealed the tomb of Hilarion in the crypt of the large church, the monastery had a number of cells, a large wall, an atrium, and an accompanying guesthouse with baths. It is reasonable to suppose that this monastery was able to sustain itself through agriculture, services to the surrounding rural community, and the hospitality to a constant flow of pilgrims. This was not an assemblage of hermits' cells, or the meeting point of lonely anchorites. It was more concentrated, more focused than Kellia. Both in terms of commodities, and of function, the monastery of Hilarion was a small city with its own hinterland, its own origin story, and its own citizens.

A Better City

The decline of the Roman city is a widespread and prominent issue with a remarkable longevity.[107] Many factors contributed to this process. It might be argued that monasteries did play a role in taking away the economic and sociopolitical pre-eminence of cities.[108] Solving the correlation between the city's decline and monasticism's surge is not the goal of this Element; but one needs to stress that monasteries were probably not the *decisive* factor in this process. Rather, they were a parallel development in many regions fulfilling the same functions.

The process of replacing cities by monasteries as hinges of local and transregional networks is by no means a given. Other options were available in Late Antiquity, like large secular or episcopal estates. But monasteries had a number of advantages. They were more reliable, they offered more stability than estates; they were more *like* cities, both on a practical and a conceptual level. They were a perfect compromise between the continuation of urban functions and the innovation in production and distribution systems. They offered solutions for a problem that a lack of cities brought: organising and regulating productive rural space. They were so successful in this respect that when we look over the chronological border of our period, especially in the West, they had essentially taken over much of what cities did in this regard even inside the urban spaces. Where monasticism met the actual desert, it has been so successful that we can call it an urbanising factor.[109] This is true even technologically – monks in the desert often had the same amenities as city dwellers.[110]

It might therefore look tempting to relate the success of one model with the decline of the other. But this is a teleological argument, and the results of both forms coexisting was never predetermined. Monasteries did not kill the Roman city. In singular cases they may have cannibalised on its foundations.

---

[107] See the variety in Salway and Drinkwater 2007.   [108] Henning 2007.
[109] Brooks Hedstrom 2017, p. 290.   [110] Tzaferis 2001, p. 320.

Sometimes the two forms competed for the same resources and their scarcity might have put them in direct competition. But those, we stress, were local and limited instances.

In fact, monasteries would often act like cities. They petitioned for tax exemptions directly to the emperor or king, they saw themselves often as being a part of the *territorium* of the imperial capital, and in many ways they were seen legally as cities. Conceptually, they started to be the 'image and likeness' of a city. Their form also often resembled that of towns. This was such a potent image that when an anonymous monk in Alemannia sketched the ideal plan for the monastery of St Gall in ca. 810, what he drew was a perfectly gridded and planned (Roman) city. The roots of this process were much earlier than the Carolingian era.

3 Monks and Nuns in the City

1. Emperors Valentinian, Theodosius, and Arcadius Augustuses to Tatianus, Praetorian Prefect
If any persons should be found in the profession of monks, they shall be ordered to seek out and to inhabit desert places and desolate solitudes.
September 2, 390

2. The same Augustuses to Tatianus, Praetorian Prefect
We direct that the monks to whom the municipalities had been forbidden, since they are strengthened by judicial injustices, shall be restored to their original status, and the aforesaid law shall be repealed. Thus indeed, We revoke such a decree of Our Clemency, and We grant them free ingress into the towns.
April 17, 392

Codex Theodosianus, 16.4.1–2.

The connection of monasticism with the city is not limited to similarities and likeness, nor to structures and group membership. Monks and nuns simply *were* in the cities. This may not have been desired by everybody. Some, like Theodosius, Valentinian, and Arcadius, tried to make them go away – but it did not even take two years for the emperors to realise that this was futile. Apparently, monasticism could not be confined to the desert. While lonely hermits certainly existed, this section will show how monasticism and asceticism were a staple of late antique city life.[111] In most cases, remarkable ascetic life was impossible without the help of the city. In fact, we can consider the preoccupation of Basil of Caesarea (329–379) with questions of praise and honour as not only touching on Christian virtues but also notions of civic recognition.[112]

---

[111] On the complicated notions of asceticism as a category, see Diem 2019.

[112] Basil of Caesarea, *Asketikon*, questions 33–36.

Eremitism and Its Audiences

After the material afterlife of Hilarion, which closed the previous section, it is tempting to have a look at his ascetic career as well. The details of this life were told by Jerome, deeply embedded in the urban world. For all the merits of desert ascesis, the fame of the great figures of monasticism relied entirely on authors and readers – for whom cities were crucial elements of their networks. This is visible in the case of Hilarion. He was revered for his asceticism and for the introduction of Egyptian-style eremitism to Palestine. Over time, he became a much-visited exorcist and miracle worker, who felt the world encroaching onto his private path to spiritual perfection.[113] This is why, in his later days, he tried to flee from both Egypt and Palestine. In a string of astonishing moves, he chose first south-eastern Sicily, then Salona in Dalmatia, and then Cyprus as refuges from the onslaught of worshippers. To his own surprise, his fame did not remain a secret in these densely populated areas. Both Sicily and Dalmatia had been heavily urbanised over the centuries of stable Roman rule. Even Hilarion's final recluse in the mountains of Cyprus was not as remote; he ended up in a regularly tended orchard.[114]

Hilarion's journey never really was about fleeing fame and followers, even if this is something that Jerome stresses.[115] It is more fruitful to think about the reasons for the apparent disconnect between words and actions: to disentangle the actions and motives of the historic Hilarion and Jerome's representation thereof. If Hilarion did travel to these places, this may have been a stunt to attract the public rather than to avoid it. After all, Jerome wrote close to Hilarion's life, so his account is bound to be less fanciful than his other *vitae* while still tailoring his literary representation for subsequent generations. It makes no sense to leave a perfectly fine desert to try and find loneliness in the outskirts of Syracuse, Salona, or Paphos. Jerome must have altered Hilarion's motives to change his perception by the audience. And although the world (and its temptations) found him everywhere he went, Hilarion still overcame all obstacles. This was an effective way of framing Hilarion's travels as a remarkable and truly monastic endeavour.

Alternatively, we can entertain the possibility that Jerome freely changed or invented the Mediterranean travels of Hilarion. The disconnect between action and motive would thus be even more pronounced. This allowed Jerome to prove two things at once through fruitful contradiction: that Hilarion was a great

---

[113] For Jerome's adaptations of biblical literature to highlight Hilarion's prowess, see Basquin-Matthey 2015.

[114] Jerome, *Life of Hilarion*, chs. 35–43. A recent analysis that also stresses Hilarion's public action is Elm 2020.

[115] Jerome, *Life of Hilarion,* chs. 30, 33, 34, 38, 39, 41, 43.

eremite and that he was *universally acclaimed* as a great eremite. And since the acclamation of some peasants in the wilderness of rocky Palestine was not worth much in the circles that interested Jerome, situating Hilarion in settings that his audience was invested in was a logical choice. Jerome did not care that strict eremitism and universal acclamation were mutually exclusive. Both furthered his cause, namely, the propagation of an exceptional monk.

Whatever we think of the amount of creative writing of Jerome, we can see how he was establishing the literary paradigm of the fleeing ascetic.[116] The inclination of his Hilarion to seek loneliness in the close vicinity of cities is not a hindrance in this respect. The conundrum sketched here is crucial for the monastic movement in general: monasteries are tied to cities by social and literary conventions and against their own rhetoric. Yet, this is also true in the lived experience of monks and nuns: the monk or nun who is driven to leave society but can never escape is a ubiquitous literary phenomenon.

The example most closely linked to Hilarion is Anthony, his teacher and literary model.[117] According Athanasius, Anthony was constantly sought out once he had gained his reputation as a lonely desert dweller. First, he founded a monastery, from which he then retired to live on a mountain – to be left alone and not to be revered.[118] There he was constantly accepting visitors, from generals to virgins, and casually corresponding with Emperor Constantine. He visited Alexandria twice, once to publicly stand up to pagan persecution, and once to fight against the Arian heresy.[119] Athanasius builds a fruitful contradiction: Anthony is both fleeing attention and seeking it. This contradiction is complemented by Anthony's stark opposition to letters and learning: he appears as illiterate, yet also propagates 'asceticism though the Scripture'.[120] This 'illiterate' Anthony was also the author of at least seven extant letters.[121] Athanasius and Jerome have the same concerns as their urban audiences. They reconcile these concerns with the ascetic ideals that lie behind the whole endeavour.

In his *Historia Religiosa*, Theodoret (393–460), bishop of Cyrus and a former monk, tells us about a certain monk Peter, a Galatian, who lived as a hermit in the outskirts of Antioch. One day, he got a surprise visit by no other than the mother of Theodoret himself. The mother learned about Peter from the wife of Pergamius, *magister militum per orientis*. That elegant lady, clad in pearls, silk and golden jewels, is chastised by Peter for wearing ostentatious

---

[116] A paradigm that would prove to be extremely successful, see John Moschus, *The Spiritual Meadow*.

[117] For the political and theological context of the *Life of Anthony*, see Cartwright 2016.

[118] Athanasius, *Life of Anthony*, ch. 49.   [119] Brennecke 2014.

[120] Athanasius, *Life of Anthony*, ch. 46.   [121] Anthony, *Letters*.

clothing – using an elaborate metaphor about late Roman portraiture.[122] The ascetic is well acquainted with the world of late Roman art. Thus, Theodoret makes it clear what kind of audience he is interested in: rich, well-educated city dwellers, who were the perfect spectators for the kerbside ascetic. It is not that important if Peter actually lived in the outskirts of a metropolis. What *is* important is that Theodoret has placed him there in his narrative. The tension between the monk withdrawn from the urban world and a rich lady of the city's elite only works in this setting. There are elements of differentiation at play but also gender representation – a male ascetic discussing art with a female aristocrat. This use of gender is a feature of Theodoret's monastic narrative.[123] To us, the knowledge that Peter has about various fashions in painting might sound absurd, but for the contemporary readers it was what they expected.

In the West, the simultaneous holding in contempt and embracing the city is the trademark of Sulpicius Severus (c. 363–425) in his life of Martin of Tours (316–397). Admittedly, Martin's legacy is in large parts due to his actions as bishop of Tours, but he was also a prime example of an ascetic who was dragged into the city (supposedly) against his will. What we know about his life and the way it was put into text by Sulpicius Severus replicates many patterns we have already encountered. Martin fled the urban environment at every turn – so *successfully* that he ended up becoming bishop of Tours. Martin was born into a solid middle-class family tied to urban and military careers, which he also followed. He deliberately left this world behind when he became an eremite. Yet, he was dependent on urban space his entire life and as we shall see, in death. Martin was not very popular among his fellow bishops due to his lack of noble background, making him even more dependent on his local urban community.[124]

After his first experiences as a hermit in Gallinara he moved to Ligugé which lay in the spiritual suburbs of Poitiers. This was a Gallo-Roman villa that Martin got as a gift from his mentor Hilary, bishop of Poitiers. His position as abbot in Ligugé also stemmed from the fact that he could build upon Hilary's personal network. Ultimately, Martin had to be tricked into accepting the bishopric of Tours. This is a literary motive similar to what authors like Jerome or Cassian do, where their protagonist's reluctance signals true monastic vocation, while also allowing for increased influence in the 'real world'.[125] Martin's tenure as bishop shows a person well-integrated in the urban milieu as well. His *coup de grace* of monasticism, the *Maius Monasterium* on the other side of the river from Tours, was said to have been 'so sheltered and remote that it did not lack

---

[122] Theoderet, *History of the Monks*, vita IX.   [123] Muehlberger 2015.   [124] Dunn 2000, p. 62.
[125] This mirrors ecclesiastical authors' difficult relationship to their previous secular 'jobs', see Burrus 1995, pp. 13–14.

Figure 7 Martin of Tours' monastery of Marmoutier just on the other side of the river from the city. Here, in an eighteenth-century painting, we can see it from the other bank. Charles-Antoine Rougeot, *Vue de l'abbaye de Marmoutier*, musée des Beaux-Arts de Tours © Musée des Beaux-Arts de Tours

the solitude of the desert'.[126] In reality, it is a half hour stroll from Marmoutier to Tours' city centre (see Figure 7).

Perhaps though the most important lesson about the audiences for monastic stories is what happened to Martin after he died. Gregory of Tours describes how the people of Poitiers and Tours fought for Martin's body: 'Ours he is as a monk, an abbot among us', said the people of Poitiers. 'But he was our bishop', replied the people of Tours, and added that if the conflict should be sorted according to where Martin was first in a monastery, then his body should go to the city of Milan. Tours won in the end because the 'almighty God did not want to deprave the city of Tours of its patron'.[127]

The effects of Tours winning the legacy of Martin would prove noticeable soon enough. Gregory tells us in his *Lives of the Fathers* about just one woman: Monegundis, a saintly hermit, and his near contemporary. She was born in Chartres, to a modestly affluent urban family, and turned her life around after the death of her two children. She chose to enclose herself in her own house, and only talk to a single maid who was to bring her flour, ashes, and water on a regular basis. However, the maid left her and Monegundis then decided to go

---

[126] Sulpicius Severus, *Life of St Martin*, chs. 10:4–5.   [127] Gregory of Tours, *Histories*, 1:48.

to Tours, to revere the relics of Martin. After tribulations and miracles, she retreated to a cell adjacent to Martin's basilica. By then she was also the head of a community of women which continued to work miracles in her name.[128] Even Sulpicius himself could not have imagined a more ideal consequence of Martin. Stories and biographies like his own would reach non-monastic, urban, and well-to-do people and lead them towards Martin's example. Urban audiences read his ascetic ventures as a suitable foil for their own situation. Even better, these people could themselves become the object of even more stories and biographies that would work in the same way. They would strengthen monastic ideals, further the monastic 'text', and furnish their movement with followers and donors. For bishops like Gregory there is an added benefit to the story because Monegundis is a case of empowerment and containment: she leaves her husband's house and hegemony and becomes empowered by Martin. But her enclosure near the basilica would ensure that her version of asceticism was always under the bishop's control.[129]

Your Neighbour, the Nun

There is a facet of monasticism that is almost too obvious to consider. Monks, nuns, and monasteries were an everyday occurrence on the streets and squares of late antique cities. You could live next to a monastery and not even notice. Athanasius gives us good insight into nuns and virgins that were everyday neighbours in late antique cities. Some of them still lived in the houses of their families or in fake marriages with male ascetics.[130] Others lived together, in a community often occupying a town house. Athanasius describes how a sisterhood of nuns went on a group pilgrimage to Jerusalem where they stayed with 'sister virgins' who operated a hostel or hospice there.[131] His letter to these sisters reads almost like a miniature rule and is clearly directed to women living in the city, under the guidance of a spiritual (female) elder. We learn about how public baths should be avoided, how to escape gossiping with (female) neighbours, and how to behave on the streets and squares of your town.[132] This is a text written for a community rooted in city life with typical urban concerns. Inhabitants of Alexandria passed the houses of these women every day, some were seen as a danger to them as well.[133] In fact, inner cities seem to have been a place where female asceticism and communal life flourished, as the liminal spaces of the outskirts were dominated by men.[134] We should not be deceived

---

[128] Gregory of Tours, *Life of Monegundis.*   [129] Coon 1997, pp. 122–6.
[130] Elm 1994, p. 336.   [131] Athanasius, *Letter to Virgins*, 1.
[132] Athanasius, *Letter to Virgins*, 15–18, 10, 14.   [133] Brakke 1995, p. 44.
[134] Elm 1994, p. 359.

by the fact that a majority of these urban nuns are anonymous to us. They clearly constituted a staple of city life in Egypt and Palestine.

Even authors that did not identify with monasticism had to face this reality. Libanius (c. 314–393), famed rhetorician and schoolmaster in fourth-century Antioch, was worried about what monks did to the pagan landscape.[135] He saw them as religious fanatics storming around and tearing down temples and statues, terrorising the peaceful population both in the countryside and in the cities.[136] Of course we do not have to take his assessment of monks as a scourge at face value. Nonetheless, his insistence that they were haunting urban religious infrastructure is telling. As a citizen of Antioch, he felt threatened by a movement he deemed new and terrifyingly destructive.

When Procopius of Caesarea (c. 500–565) described the role of monks in the fall of Amida in the sixth century, things did not look so special anymore.[137] As a classicising historian, Procopius pretended to be unfamiliar with the concept of monks, but he was ready to mock their main characteristic. These monks were partly responsible for the fall of the city to the Persians because, for once, they were not adhering to a strict diet, but feasted at the occasion of a Christian holiday. Consequently, they were so sleepy the night of the attack that they failed to warn the defenders. Procopius was not a pagan author, but his archaic style of writing lent itself well to attesting to the normalcy of monks in Roman cities while pretending not to know anything about monasticism. For his audience, monks getting drunk in a city must have been an amusing but not improbable anecdote.

That is all fine in the heavily urbanised Eastern Empire, but what about the West? The sermons gathered in an anonymous fifth-century collection, the *Eusebius Gallicanus,* draw direct parallels between monastic and urban communities, presenting them as dealing with the same problems.[138] Monastic life was conceptualised in the same way as the everyday life of townspeople. Later, Pope Gregory the Great's writings demonstrate the widespread acceptance of monks as townspeople,[139] though cities found themselves under a far greater demographic pressure and an overall contraction of urban space was commonplace. Plenty of Gregory's many correspondents were urban abbots and many of his letters concern monks and monasteries in cities. The 'urban danger' to monasticism was not a factor in his world, monks and monasteries integrated in cities. Gregory's Rome boasted 3,000 nuns and monks alone.[140] A longing for an idealised eremitic past of monasticism might underpin Gregory's pastoral and monastic writings but the practicalities of a lived monastic experience from

---

[135] For an introduction to Libanius, see Cribiore 2007.   [136] Libanius, *Orations*, n. 30.8–10.
[137] Procopius, *Wars*, I.7. For Procopius, see Lillington-Martin and Turquois 2017.
[138] See Bailey 2006.   [139] On Gregory and his role, see Markus 1981; Demacopoulos 2015.
[140] Wood 2022, p. 46.

Britain to Constantinople (the extent of his network) show that while monks and cities remained sometimes in tension, they cannot be seen as opposites. The city in Gregory shows itself as a place of control: the wandering monks in Sicily, uprooted by war and devastation, were to go to Messina. This was due to concerns about the image that begging and idle monks might produce of the church, and concerns about how to control the monks. They were to be sought out and gathered in the city, where the bishop would make sure that they returned to life according to their rule.[141]

Gregory was not alone in his concerns. Fructuosus (ca. 595–665), prolific monastic author and bishop of Braga, observed how men, women, children, and even slaves were forming monastic communities in their town houses. This practice he criticised in the harshest of tones – not for their lack of seclusion in the desert, but for their ignorance of his, Fructuosus', episcopal oversight.[142] These people were congregating horizontally, binding themselves by oath to each other, and never even requested their bishop's permission.[143] For Gregory, vertical control via the bishop was paramount as well. He was worried that monks were still being sued in civic courts. He wanted them to be under ecclesiastical authority. This hints once again at the fact that monks and nuns had initially been treated as an issue for secular law. The move to an episcopal court would not have meant a removal from urban space either – the bishops' jurisdictions would of course also include cities.[144] The pope relied on men like a certain Secundus, a papal emissary to Ravenna established in this city, to receive information about other courts than his own. Secundus was – of course – a monk.[145] There is also Gregory's abode. He had established a monastery for himself and his companions on Caelio, one of the seven hills of Rome, and functioned in an urban environment once he had become pope. For him it seemed natural to rely on monasticism as an urban phenomenon. This was the place where monks were most useful to him, politically, and over which he had the most control. He wanted monasticism to be represented in cities. He acknowledged monasteries 'in the desert', as he wrote to one Palladius in a monastery on Mount Sinai, but he did not see any substantial spiritual differences between city and desert, for 'the ancient enemy is not excluded from tempting humankind in any land'.[146]

Monasticism Coming to Terms with the City

So far, we have acknowledged that monasticism's earliest proponents had never left the city behind, and that monks and nuns had become an accepted feature of

---

[141] Gregory the Great, *Letters*, 1.39.   [142] See Diaz 2018.
[143] Fructuosus, *General Rule*, ch. 1.   [144] Gregory the Great, *Letters*, 6.11.
[145] Gregory the Great, *Letters*, 6.23, 33, 7.10.   [146] Gregory the Great, *Letters*, 11.1.

urban spaces by the sixth century. What we are lacking is an inspection of monasticism actively dealing with its fateful relationship to the city. For this we can turn to a pair of authors of the fifth and sixth centuries: Rabbula of Edessa (fl. 411–435) and Caesarius of Arles (c. 470–542). Both were monks-turned-bishops, on different ends of the Mediterranean. Their lives and careers already hint at the potential internal conflicts that we can find in their writing.

Rabbula's anonymous biographer wrote a couple of decades later, perhaps coming from the next generation of Edessenian clerics. Rabbula was born in a small town called Chalcis not far from Beroia (modern-day Aleppo).[147] He believed in pagan deities before turning to Christianity, and became a city magistrate, coming from a wealthy family background. After his conversion the bishops of Chalcis and Beroia convinced him to live as a monk. He swore to 'abandon the world completely',[148] went on a pilgrimage and settled down in a monastery near Chalcis. He sold all his goods, freed his slaves, divorced his wife, and put his mother and his children into the care of another monastery. He soon attracted visitors and admirers – whom he fled by becoming a solitary hermit in the inner desert, like his role model Anthony. We can see how Rabbula's life is shaped by the literary movement. He was also traced and found by his monastic fellows. Then, ignoring his will to leave the world, he went to Baalbek with a companion and publicly denounced the pagans. This is again an emulation of Anthony and his visit to Alexandria to denounce the heretics. Both were seeking martyrdom yet were spared. Both left the world for good, yet chose a big, urban, stage to profess their creed.

Once he was elected bishop of Edessa in 411, Rabbula started a campaign to transform the city and its monastic landscape (see Figure 8). His hagiographer stresses that Rabbula wanted to stop all episcopal building activities in Edessa.[149] His own monastic rule limited the free movement of monks and cut their involvement into everyday lay activities.[150] It seems that Rabbula saw the city as an antagonist, as something that should disappear and not disturb the minds and souls of good Christians. The only thing he apparently cared for were the poor, and the controlled ascesis of his monks. It is critical, however, to put his actions into their proper context.

As with all hagiographic texts, we should be wary of the hagiographer's agenda. Aristocratic wealth and its transfer to the poor is a recurrent theme of the text. Rabbula's familial wealth and status are highlighted to make his conversion to asceticism more pronounced. But Rabbula was just one actor in

---

[147] For an introduction to Rabbula, see Phenix and Horn 2017, pp. xvii–cclviii.
[148] *Life of Rabbula*, 2, 7.   [149] Leppin 2020, p. 192.
[150] Rabbula, *Adm. Mon.*, 1, 2, 5, 6, 15, 22, 23.

Figure 8 Jesus, beleaguered by monks in a sixth-century manuscript of the Rabbula Gospels. Firenze, Biblioteca Medicea Laurenziana, Ms. Plut. 1.56, c. 14r, Su concessione del MiC. È vietata ogni ulteriore riproduzione con qualsiasi mezzo

conflict-ridden Edessa. His vision of 'pure' Christian belief and praxis stood in opposition to the aristocratic circles that had dominated the city with their politics and their self-representation. Rabbula's successor Ibas (fl. 435–457) was backed by this aristocratic faction, and was all too ready to discredit Rabbula, on grounds both theological (Ibas would later become infamous as one of the three 'chapters' that the second council of Constantinople banned) and societal.[151] Before he was bishop, Ibas led the School of Edessa, a position formally subordinated to the bishop, yet also the nucleus of a network of important clergymen. Ibas becoming Rabbula's successor was a logical step that ensured the autonomy of the school, its theology, and the aristocratic-leaning clergy that supported them. The hagiographer was therefore also part of the controversy, and his text should be understood as anti-aristocratic in this sense.[152] When the text claims that Rabbula never used any money to build something in the city, it should be read as a rejection of the classical practice of noble civic euergetism. And in fact, we do see him investing money in the building of almshouses for both men and women.[153] Rabbula is portrayed as transforming the role of the city towards the ideal Christian one, where the rich and powerful (including the bishop) would spend their money to help the poor, without any representative inclination. Rabbula could well have been a proponent of a new euergetism that favoured (ecclesiastically controlled) monasticism and its ideals. His natural enemy was Ibas as champion of trad-itionally aristocratic interests.[154] Rabbula's vision was not so different from John Chrysostom's vision of Antioch as a city of household 'monasteries', focusing on the city's Great Church.[155] The city was to be like a monastery (which in turn was closely based on a city, as we have seen with Kellia). This feedback loop paved the way to a new understanding of Christian urbanism.

A narrative mechanism is at play in Rabbula's rules for monks as well.[156] They must be read as part of a larger discourse about the state of integration of monks into lay society. These rules tell us in the first place that monks were part of the social fabric of cities. Rabbula forbids individual monks to visit inns, get treatment in hospitals, give testimony in judicial courts, buy and sell at markets, and attend lay burial ceremonies. He would not have forbidden actions that nobody considered doing. His concern was with monasticism's distinction and its role in the city. As with the aristocratic circles and their habits, Rabbula wanted monks to refrain from certain behaviours normal to most contemporar-ies. In the same vein, he also condemned monks who possessed books 'outside of the faith of the church' – or their own horse. He was writing rules for men

---

[151] Ibas and Rabbula were arguing heavily over the condemnation of Theodore of Mopsuestia in the early 430s. See Phenix and Horn 2017, pp. clxxvii–clxxviii.

[152] Leppin 2020, p. 191.   [153] *Life of Rabbula*, 50.

[154] A similar conclusion in Drijvers 1996, pp. 245–7.   [155] Brown 1988, p. 313.

[156] Three different, but overlapping rules have survived to date, see Phenix and Horn 2017, p. ccxxii.

who had not changed much of their lifestyle when they had become monks. Added to his desire for monastic distinction was also his episcopal drive to control the monks. The precept that monks were to abstain from trading relics makes a lot of sense: monks were acting individually with spiritual objects and capital, without the supervision of the bishop. The apparent spread of these characteristics and behaviours in his diocese led to the design of very short *regulae*, lacking many of the typical aspects of the genre but weirdly specific in limiting the social role of the monks. Rabbula tried to reverse the existing symbiosis of monasticism and urbanism in Edessa, ultimately but predictably failing. His radical programme collapsed on many fronts: he was superseded by a bishop of less radical views concerning monks and lay society. His views were evidently not popular. Neither his rules nor his vita created a stable invented tradition that following generations of monks and bishops in Edessa were ready to fall back on.

The literary unease with the city is also a common trope for Caesarius, bishop of Arles from 502 to 542. He was ready to use anti-urban metaphors in his writings. In an exemplary sermon he stated that the 'worldly city' was where good Christians labour but are unhappy. Prideful monks, on the other hand, would be thrown into the 'city of the devil'.[157] He made sure to close all the gates of the nunnery that he had founded in Arles, to prevent external influences.[158] Caesarius's attitudes stem from his time as a monk in Lérins, a monastery that remained mistrustful of the outside world and itself was anything but an urban centre.[159] Situated on an island off the southern coast of modern-day France, Lérins was geographically remote from urban centres. But this did not make the island a recluse: Lérins had supplied a whole generation of Gallic bishops and Caesarius was, in essence, a product of a 'monk to city bishop' pipeline with a tradition spanning as far back as Hilary of Arles (c. 403–449) and the monastery's founder Honoratus (c. 350–429). The latter two became bishops of Arles as well. For both, coming to the city was the logical conclusion to their monastic lives – the desert was but a phase.[160] The city is not an antinomy here – it is the last career stage.

Caesarius uses the genre-typical mistrustful language but remains committed to monasticism in the urban context in practice. In fact, Arles served a picturesque backdrop in Caesarius' *Vita*. His monastery for nuns is founded first in the spiritual suburb of Arles, and then refounded in the city after it was destroyed in the aftermath of the war in 507/508 to provide better protection.[161] Caesarius gets chastised by the pope for selling church property to fund his

---

[157] Caesarius, *Sermons*, n. 151, 233.   [158] Caesarius, *Rule for Nuns*, ch. 73.
[159] For Lérins, see Codou and Lauwers 2009.   [160] Leyser 1991, pp. 96–7.
[161] *Life of Caesarius*, book 1, c. 35.

monastery. Yet, his nunnery is adjacent to the former cathedral, linked with it by a door never to be opened and entrusted, in a move to ensure family fortunes, first to his sister Caesaria the Elder and then to his niece, Caesaria the Younger. With the establishment of the nunnery in the city comes not only the feeling of safety, the integration with the visible structure of the city, but also its invisible, sociopolitical fabric. For obvious reasons, then, is his rule for nuns engaging civic behaviour. It limits displays of civic duties and status, both from the nuns itself, and from potential visitors, and other urban actors.

Caesarius' monastic practice is fully capable of functioning within the context of Roman urban space because this is the tradition he is coming from. He knows the mechanisms of urban life just as well as those of the aristocracy and he can delineate the lives of nuns and monks accordingly. But it is nonetheless obvious that monasticism for him was never meant to leave both concepts behind entirely: status and the city were to be regulated, but they were also a reality Caesarius was ready to accept.

A paradox appears: building a cloistered female community inside a city is bound to cause numerous problems that could be avoided outside of it.[162] The ideal separation, the distance to worldly temptations or the avoidance of interference from the city's rich and mighty (all problems that Caesarius tries to tackle in his rule) are much easier to achieve if you just move away. But the advantages of the integration with the urban fabric outweigh the possible points of friction. In a way, this friction is also a literary opportunity: it requires a written rule that will develop strategies to deal with said frictions, both real and theoretical. It also creates the potential for distinction and highlights moral and theological superiority of said community. Ultimately, placing the nunnery inside the city solidifies the rule as an invented tradition. Caesarius' rule achieved that goal – abbess Rusticula (d. c. 632) still ran the place according to his rule in the seventh century.[163] The nunnery was to be a place where women were governing themselves without the influence of men. It was also a place of learning, a path to the fulfilment of the ideal learned Christian woman. Caesarius' vision is clear: 'Let them all learn to read. And in all times they should spend two hours, that is from dawn to the second hour, on reading.'[164]

Worried about the fate of his most cherished creation, Caesarius commends the nunnery not only to the protection of the future bishops, but to the entire city of Arles. After his death, Arles was to stand guardian over Caesarius' nuns (see Figure 9). The city itself, understood in a late Roman sense as a familial unity of 'the clergy, the office of the prefect, the counts, and the citizens',[165] replaces

---

[162] Tilley 2018.   [163] *Life of Rusticula*, ch. 10.   [164] Caesarius, *Rule for Nuns*, chs. 18–19.
[165] *Life of Caesarius*, ch. 47, p. 64.

Figure 9 Arles was place of one of the most interesting monastic experiments of late antiquity: Caesarius' monastery for virgins. Photo: Mateusz Fafinski

Caesarius as the caregiver of the nunnery. A monastery becomes finally integrated into the urban *familia*.

Caesarius and Rabbula show us that strict anti-urban rhetoric is not determined by career and upbringing. Both knew the positives of the city and both had profited from urban settings. Yet neither Caesarius nor Rabbula held back their fervour against urban amenities. Social distinction had benefitted both, yet they pleaded to prevent all kinds of gatherings where their monks and nuns might profit from their own or see other people's social status.

Nevertheless, there must be a limit to rhetoric: if you try too hard to make your rhetoric a reality, the tension between your ideal and the situation on the ground will become too great to bear. But tension is necessary for monasticism's relationship with the city in Late Antiquity: it guarantees distinction and keeps the monastic movement on its toes. Caesarius seems to understand that well – he knows the limits of the material with which he works. Hence his strategy is ultimately successful and long-standing. Rabbula seems to have driven the tension beyond the breaking point. His rules, fragmentary and disjointed as they were, and the testimony of his vita paint a picture of someone who did not see the limits of his own rhetoric. Preciously little remained in practice after Rabbula died and his successor Ibas had taken over. The community and the monks were apparently not euphoric about Rabbula's programme of applying anti-urban and anti-social rhetoric in practice. Such rhetoric can uphold a movement only if those who use it know how far they can take it.

Gangs of New Jerusalem

John Moschus (c. 550–619) relates in his *Spiritual Meadow* (written in a city, in Rome) how the whole spiritual philosophy of a certain abba Marcellus was based on his experience in the circus. When Marcellus was young, he witnessed in his hometown of Apamea how famed charioteer Phileremos ('lover of the wilderness'; the whole analogy is laid on rather thick) failed to win an important race. The crowd of his frantic fans began to chant 'Phileremos takes no prize in [this] city.' From that day on, Marcellus, every time he felt the need to go to the city, would tell himself 'Marcellus, Phileremos takes no victor's crown in the city.' And this strategy worked for thirty-five years until his monastery was devastated by invaders and he was sold into slavery.[166] Should we be surprised that Marcellus was more motivated to stay in the monastery by what is in essence a pretty good sport anecdote than by some pious writings of the desert fathers? We can see him, murmuring under his breath 'Marcellus! Phileremos takes no victor's crown in the city!' as he paces the courtyard of his monastery just as today an ambitious young athlete might put a poster on their wall with the Michael Jordan quote 'You must expect great things of yourself before you can do them.' We should not, therefore, be surprised for Marcellus is of course both, the abbot and the charioteer 'lover of the wilderness'. He might have left the physical urban space, but his point of reference remained in the city. Deep down he was a product of the circus-going urban crowd – and of urban politics.[167]

Marcellus takes us to a different place: to a world where monks and nuns appear as group protagonists in urban politics. Marcellus is not only actively trying to get away from the races. He is also stopping himself from getting involved in the movement behind the races: the circus factions. And with them inevitably came local, and imperial, politics. In a world where questions of succession, disputes about faith, and fights for regional autonomy became more and more entangled, monasticism was quickly made into a civic force.

In the East, monks were connected with urban political factions and the disturbances that followed from their discontent. Monks were present both in the city crowds asking for the deposition of Ibas – Rabbula's rival and successor in Edessa – as well as in the judicial proceedings leading to his (short-lived)

---

[166] John Moschus, *The Spiritual Meadow*, ch. 152.

[167] Strikingly, even Jerome's Hilarion interacted with the races, miraculously stopping the pagan team's chariot. Jerome, *Life of Hilarion*, ch. 20.

deposition in 449. The report of the imperial *comes* Chareas before the synod of Ephesus in 449 treats monks as an integral part of Edessa's society.[168]

Monasticism's notorious involvement in education and church politics played a role in the events that led to the destruction of the Serapeum in 391.[169] Monastic influence was also felt in the anti-pagan actions in Alexandria in 486. Monks played a heavy role in the disturbances in Antioch in 511 and 512, and in the prelude to the Nika Riot in 531.[170] On the pages of Cyril of Scythopolis (c. 525–559), the Sabaite movement's unofficial record-keeper, historian, and apologist, we meet gangs of monks fighting in the streets of Jerusalem with hired cut-throats, including an appearance of rather mysterious Thracian monks.[171] We also learn that in about 513, the current archbishop made an alliance with the monks of St Sabas and St Theodore to deny the combined will of Severus of Antioch and emperor Anastasius. In the end, their alliance overcame the *dux palaestinae* and repelled Severus with supposedly 10,000 monks and the support of the emperor's nephew Hypatius. The riot was successful: the emperor was furious, but too busy to react with force, and had to accept the victory of the bishop and his monastic following.

Monks did not press their will against the empire alone. Instead, one should look towards the involvement of local officials who were eager to preserve their own interests, and the intersection of court politics through Hypatius, ecclesiastical politics (the dioceses of Antioch and Jerusalem fighting for supremacy), and of course theology. Crucially, however, Cyril voluntarily built up the role of his desert monks in this decidedly urban affair. He *wanted* to portray his brothers as a civic force, able to shut down an imperial magistrate, and to gather for an assembly in Jerusalem. It is less relevant for us whether the Sabaites actually made the difference. They claimed for themselves to be an urban faction, while never losing sight of their status as a community that had retreated from this world and embraced the desert.

Monks and nuns shared then many features with other urban 'groups of influence'.[172] Even if they were living outside of the city walls, that did not stop them from taking part in city politics. These sorts of troubles antedate the Council of Chalcedon in 451 – troubles that likely played their part in triggering the first episcopal regulation concerning monks.[173] A prominent example of this is the epic struggle between John Chrysostom, in his function as patriarch of Constantinople, and one Isaac, leader of the capital's monastic faction.

---

[168] *Acts of the Synod of Ephesus in 449*, pp. 15–55.   [169] Watts 2010, p. 14.
[170] Evagrius Scholasticus, *Church History*, book 3, ch. 32; John Malalas, *Chronicle*, book 18, ch. 71.
[171] Cyril of Scythopolis, *Lives of the Monks of Palestine*, 193.23–194.13.   [172] Hatlie 2006.
[173] Events brought to the point in Caner 2002, pp. 190–205.

Monks had been established in the capital for several decades before, and they had played their part in the regional offshoot of the Arian controversy. At the start of the fifth century, however, things began to get out of hand for the highest figure of the imperial church. Isaac seems to have been born into an unknown family in the Aramaic east. Chrysostom's close acquaintance Palladius called him a little Syrian knave.[174] For the Greek-speaking upper class, this alone was probably reason enough to wish Isaac's influence in Constantinople be minimal. Yet worse, Isaac took sides in a highly charged affair: the patriarch of Alexandria had successfully lobbied to depose Chrysostom in 403, with the support of Constantinopolitan monks.[175] Even though Chrysostom soon regained his position, he was keen to get back at those who had undermined him. Especially so, since the monks had rioted after his return, and killed several of the patriarch's followers. Tensions were relaxing only after both Isaac and Chrysostom left the city in the following year.

The most glaring issue between them had been on a structural level. Isaac had acquired the patronage of important noblemen after Theodosius, who had built him a monastery in the spiritual suburbs, had officially 'ended' Arianism. In the following years, Isaac continued to court his benefactors, and established himself as almsgiver and caretaker of the poor on their behalf. He stayed until late at aristocratic parties to raise money, which he then spent on his underprivileged following and the poor masses. This may sound like a noble undertaking, but John Chrysostom saw himself threatened by a movement that had established itself as a hinge between the wealthy city elites and the people, bypassing the church structures altogether. The patriarch watched his practical and spiritual authority waning – in his own backyard! He consequently preached against the pastoral care that monks gave (something he had done already in Antioch in the years prior), and tried to monopolise hospitals and other, formerly monastic, institutions. However, the monks were not priests and he could not bind them to his ecclesiastical rule.

Monastic leaders like Isaac were promoting the incorporation of their movement into the city's social fabric. The mechanism of patronage was a key element. It allowed the monks to acquire a dependent clientele below, and to appear as useful clients above. City magnates could therefore see monks as spiritually useful, but also as ready tools to manage mass engagement. This trick would prove useful in the turbulent years immediately before the Council of Chalcedon. Bishops like Dalmatius and Eutyches had caught on and understood their own role as patrons. They consequently turned Chrysostom's rejection of

---

[174] Palladius, *Dialogue on the Life of John Chrysostom*, ch. 6.
[175] For this affair see Elm 1998.

monks around, and instead utilised their numbers and discipline to showcase their public support and to intimidate their ecclesiastical opponents.

After Chalcedon, Isaac's business-model would get ruled out, as monks were placed under the *aegis* of their bishop. After emperor Justinian's further interventions in the sixth century at the latest it would be impossible to stir up monks or nuns against the bishop in a similar fashion.[176] By that time it had become clear to everybody that monasticism was part of city life. The inhabitants of the monasteries inside and outside of the city walls were engrained in its social relations and its daily politics. They were yet another group to account for in the handling of Late Antiquity's complex urbanity.

The West leaves us dearly wanting when it comes to urban-monastic factions even if monks and monasteries quickly gained political and ecclesiastical influence. There are but traces of their possible subversive activity, and those are in sources as unreliable as the early *Liber Pontificalis* which is hard to be trusted before the sixth century. Pope Hormisdas (514–523) through his legates Ennodius and Pelegrinus apparently used a network of monks dispersed in different cities of the empire to distribute his nineteen letters of faith under the very nose of emperor Anastasius. If we are to trust this account, it tells us little about the monks in the West, but it does confirm that the pope could rely on thoroughly urban-monastic networks to defend his vision of orthodoxy. The chronicles in Gaul, Spain, or North Africa tell us little about local city politics, and even less about possible monastic factions. We do get some glimpses though. Gregory of Tours described a mutiny by the nuns of Poitiers against their abbess. The nuns left their monastery and moved from one city to another, from Poitiers to Tours, where Gregory helped them. Finally, they stormed their monastery in Poitiers together with a band of 'thieves, killers, libertines and every sort of criminal'.[177] Marius of Avenches described in his chronicle how in 565 a group of monks from St Maurice d'Agaune tried to kill their bishop Agricola over a privileges dispute and how a pitched battle developed between the 'citizens' and the monks.[178] Additionally, surely there were groups of wandering ascetics or spiritual beggars, who might have considered themselves monks. The rule of Benedict of Nursia in the sixth century lists two species of them, differentiating between the behaviour of legitimate monks and other 'obscure' ascetics.[179] These groups might have been partly an urban phenomenon as well. In the variety of socio-religious movements prior to the

---

[176] Hasse-Ungeheuer 2016, p. 142.

[177] Gregory of Tours, *Histories*, IX, 40; see also Dailey 2015, pp. 64–79.

[178] Marius of Avenches, *Chronicle*, ad annum 565.

[179] *The Rule of Benedict*, I, 1–10. The exercise to find and name 'heretical' monks was common, see Jerome's 'remnuoth' in Jerome, *Letters*, Ep. 22, ch. 24.

institutionalisation of monasticism, the West did probably not differ much from the East. But monks as a coalesced urban faction are not to be found in the late antique and early medieval West.

All in all, the image we get is of monks and nuns being integrated in the urban fabric already in the early fifth century, and progressively gaining in importance. Both urban monks and monks of the spiritual suburbs played their role in the urban politics of the late antique East. Sometimes their behaviour was similar to the circus factions and resembled that of violent mobs.[180] Their presence in this urban context was perhaps surprising at first; what they tried to achieve in practice was not. In the West, the political culture and the urban fabric began to differ from the eastern examples before monasticism developed into a 'force in the streets'. Its political impact was to be more subtle but no less important.

A great story in the life of Saint Lupicinus (composed in Gaul in the early sixth century) illustrates well how the tables had turned. A certain count Agrippinus must go to Rome in order to save his skin (of course with the spiritual help of Lupicinus). Due to a series of unfortunate events, he finds himself on the run from prison on the streets of Rome. Desperately wanting to get to Saint Peter's, he asks a monk on the street for the shortest route. The monk duly obliges and seeing that Agrippinus cannot navigate the city at all gives him detailed instructions and tells him about 'all the squares and intersections he would have to cross; since Agrippinus was ignorant of these places, the monk left no detail of the correct route uncertain'.[181] Now it is the monk who shows a count around the city. And not just any city – Rome itself.

4 Monastic Learning

> *No one is permitted to stand up and to make a party, quarrel and confusion about*
> *something that was right. And whosoever is found that he does one of these*
> *(things), and stands up against the truth and disputes, shall receive punishment.*
> *He shall become foreign to the community and the residence in the town.*
>
> *Canons of the School of Nisibis, 1.*

During the excavations in the monastery of Epiphanius in Thebes in the early twentieth century, hundreds of ostraca and papyri fragments were found. They paint a picture of a busy monastic centre, concerned with local and broader imperial matters alike. Among the wills, letters, and fragments of liturgical texts, we also find traces of a monastic school. One ostracon from the end of the sixth century shows four repetitions of the first line of the Iliad.[182] Someone had exercised copying this line.

---

[180] Cameron 1976.   [181] *Life of Lupicinus*, c. 104.
[182] Met 14.1.140 published in Crum and Evelyn White 1926, p. 320, pl. XIV.

Those and similar fragments are an indication of educational activity.[183] Prospective monks in Egypt did have a chance to receive at least an elementary education before they entered the monastery.[184] They also continued educational activities afterwards or at least had an opportunity to do so.[185] The evidence of classical texts being used might be limited, but the sheer amount of other documentary evidence points to a developed chirographic practice in monasteries both in the West and in the East.

Many avenues of research tried to frame monastic education in terms of a continuation of classical *paideia*. This is, of course, a logical step and one that would show a direct link between urban and monastic modes of education. Education in classical antiquity was a largely urban endeavour – schools, teachers, and clients were centred around cities. While education was surely to be had in rural estates as well, it remained tied to the city.

But the relatively uneven distribution of evidence and a wide variety of adaptation strategies throughout the Broad Mediterranean make this approach through *paideia* limiting. Instead, we explore various currents that connected monastic education with the city. How did monks and nuns learn to read and write, and why did they need to do so in the first place? We will frame the issue as a convergence of two related phenomena: civic (meaning urban and secular) and monastic education, featuring unlikely siblings – two schools on the opposite ends of the Broad Mediterranean. As we will see, the monastery was simultaneously an iteration of and an alternative to civic learning.

We Don't Need No Education?

Monastic rules give us major insight into how various authors imagined the functioning of monasticism as a genre of society as well as into their authors' expectations of what kind of people their monks and nuns would or should be. For Augustine, deeply rooted in the 'elite monastic withdrawal',[186] literacy was something of a given – he could hardly imagine his educated monks living without books. In his *Praeceptum*, he does not stipulate how monks should learn to read and write (something he takes for granted) but rather wishes to organise how they ask for books.[187] The same expectation underpins numerous Latin rules. The early Gallic *Second Rule of the Fathers* in the fifth century reserves time for reading,[188] and St Benedict in the sixth assumes enough knowledge of reading that each monk would be able to read aloud.[189] Shenoute informs us that

---

[183] Maravela 2018, pp. 133–7, 147.   [184] Cribiore 1996, pp. 3–34, 129–52.
[185] See Larsen and Rubenson 2018.   [186] Bruning 2001.
[187] *Rule of Augustine*, Praeceptum VI.10.
[188] Second Rule of the Fathers 5.23 in *The Rules of the Fathers*.
[189] *The Rule of Benedict*, IX.

the default mode of communication between male and female communities was of course through letters.[190] He naturally assumed a level of practical literacy among both monks and nuns.

Even in the Egyptian desert and in the milieu of the first-generation of monks, it appears that Anthony was literate. He knew enough Greek to understand the complicated writings of Origen – even if his biographer Athanasius stressed that he tried to stay away from schools and books.[191] This, of course, does not mean that all monks and nuns were able to read and write. They also did not necessarily take part in any literary activity, passively or actively. But it does show that monks were *expected* to be educated enough to do so. The reality might have been less uniform in this regard, more along the lines of 'many were called, few were chosen'. Nevertheless, for a movement that depended so much on the effects of literarisation, this expectation had to have been at least partly fulfilled. It was by no means a coincidence that the highly literate Anthony became the model for so many monastic ideas.

Christian and civic education did, at least in part, happen in the same places. Initially, their shared space was the urban space. Authors like Jerome, Augustine, or John Chrysostom attended urban schools of rhetoric, and although they postured a lot later on to gain a form of literalised distance (when they switched their societal genre from bureaucrats to theologians), their education was that of the urban elite. But this common position of urban and Christian education was not limited to bishops or theologians. A whole strand of institutions shared elements of monastic character with the framework of a rhetoric or philosophy school. Already Didymus the Blind in fourth-century Alexandria was seen as an ascetic leading a quasi-monastic community, even if he remained technically a layman all his life.[192] Didymus went on to educate a whole generation of thinkers, among them Palladius, Rufinus, and Jerome. If we look closely, we see an entire section of quasi-monastic practices connected with cities, which greatly influenced monasticism's maturity. And yet we note that this urban-based, grammar-school-framed form of education was already becoming Christianised in the fourth century. The Tura Papyri, which contain works of Didymus and questions from students, show that grammar was taught using Christian writings and the Old Testament.[193] One did not have to leave the city and the grammar school to get an education based on Christian texts. While monks and nuns might have had a varied level of literacy, those who wrote down their stories and shaped their image in the imagination of subsequent generations were certainly literate.

---

[190] Shenoute, *Rules*, no. 426.   [191] Wipszycka 2014, pp. 66–72.
[192] Layton 2004, pp. 13–14.   [193] Stefaniw 2018.

Civic and Monastic Frames of Education

In the West, Julius Pomerius (fl. c. 500) is a prime example of blurring lines between monastic and civic education. He is a bit of an enigma in the world of late antique and early medieval monasticism. Coming from North Africa, he was a grammarian and a teacher of rhetoric, who finally settled in Arles. In Gaul, he was probably ordained a priest. His contemporaries praised him and among his correspondents were Ruricius of Limoges and Ennodius of Pavia, both of whom tried to convince him to visit their cities. His 'educational practice' in Arles attracted aristocratic pupils. It is hard to think about a personage better integrated with the urban tissue of the late fifth century. He wrote his own spiritual guide, *De vita contemplativa,* arguing for a shift of a model for clerics and bishops alike – they should be less aristocrats and more monks.[194] He corresponded with Ruricius, who saw him as a spiritual guide, referring to him, with typical hyperbole, as 'lord of his soul' and abbot.[195] The confusion about the status of his establishment has led some to believe he was an abbot already in Africa.[196] His school attracted monks – Caesarius landed there after his stint at Lérins[197] – and in general, seemed to have existed conceptually between a monastic community and a school of rhetoric. This form seemed to have been not only acceptable but also praiseworthy for leading clerics of the day.

There is no fundamental contradiction between the urban and monastic aspects of Pomerius' initiative in Arles. The dichotomy is purely rhetorical. His writings and his monastic praxis in the city engage with the crucial aspect of monastic vocation. Those who can devote their lives to seek salvation full time – that is, monks and nuns – have a responsibility for other Christians. They need to look for them and care for their spiritual well-being there where they can be found, also in towns. Monks had to follow rules but could also engage in pastoral care. This notion will have a great impact on writings of people like Gregory the Great and his *Regula Pastoralis* but also later in works like those of Chrodegang and other Carolingian writers.[198] The city was not simply a pragmatic choice but an element of the salvific mission.

Pomerius' enterprise is remarkable. We have here a classical rhetorician and grammarian from North Africa, running a school for wealthy urban and rural aristocrats in Arles of the 490s, who wrote manuals of ascetic living. The author of the *vita* of one of his pupils, Caesarius, displays true shock and horror at Pomerius's views and the curriculum of his school. Clearly there was not only

---

[194] Julianus Pomerius, *The Contemplative Life.*   [195] Ruricius, *Letters,* Ep. 2, 10, 1.17.
[196] Fick 2011, pp. 198–9.   [197] Klingshirn 1994, pp. 72–82; Leyser 2006, pp. 65–100.
[198] Leyser 2000, pp. 161–2.

some 'worldly knowledge' involved but also Augustine.[199] And it is all fine! Bishops write to him, monks attend his school, his works are read and copied. The city is not only a place where a manual of ascetic life can be written; it is also a place where monks can come for learning. The fact that the author of the *Vita Caesarii* utilised the well-known literary trope of a justifying dream for Caesarius' residence with Pomerius is wholly appropriate. This was a form of literary polemic, stylised after the example of Jerome in the desert, and further shows how literarisation fuelled monasticism's rhetoric of distinction. The city and its urban institutions were necessary antagonists and essential partners.

Looking East, education and learning seem to have been a sphere where even those monks most vocal in their critique of the city seem to allow monastic presence in towns. 'This very Ganus tells us then that you are living in a monastery and that if you ever come into town, it is only to consult books, and so much of their contents as pertains to theology', writes Synesius of Cyrene.[200] This is not surprising at all – where else should the monks come for books? The sheer logistics of late fourth-century Cyrenaica (and other provinces) meant that one needed to go to the city occasionally. The alternatives – burgeoning monasteries in the spiritual suburbs – were at least at the beginning not numerous and not focused on copying enough to produce a steady stream of books. This was to change in the upcoming centuries, but even this change also had to do with cities.[201] We can already see that cities produced ascetic and Christian forms of communal living that were half a step from traditional urban schools of rhetoric. The curricula of those establishments seem to have been mixed in content. They were founded where the books and the teachers were – in the cities. But this is more than just about books and teachers: it is about an intermediate form of monasticism between a school and a monastery. This form has hardly a more prominent example than the School of Nisibis.

This centre of learning moving between Nisibis and Edessa and between the Roman Empire and Persia from the mid-fourth to the early seventh century, is an extraordinary example of the diversity of monastic-like practices in the city.[202] As an institution, it was an urban phenomenon that adopted progressively stringent forms of monastic behaviour but never lost its urban roots. At some point, probably towards the mid-sixth century, it developed monastic rules for its students while never changing their status to 'full' monks.[203] They could come to the school for a fixed period and pursue other interests during their

---

[199] *Life of Caesarius*, ch. 9. See also Diem 2021, p. 295, showing that it was Pomerius who was responsible for Augustine's importance in Caesarius' life and teachings.

[200] Synesius, *Letters*, 147.   [201] Cassiodorus, *Institutions*, I.30.1.

[202] See Vööbus 1965, pp. 90–114, 177–209.   [203] *The Statutes of the School of Nisibis*.

holidays.[204] Lest this shock us, we know that in Egypt, for example, early monks left their monasteries to get some money on the side helping with harvest or other agricultural work.[205] The school was always a hub for the closely-knit network of the Eastern church, a 'common mother' of its most prominent protagonists,[206] proving again that the church, monasticism and urbanism were inseparable elements in a durable system that would continue to thrive even after the Islamic conquest.[207] There is a remarkable unity of the 'town and community' in the Statutes of the School of Nisibis. The phrase 'expelled from the community and from the town' in various wordings appears in it ten times.[208]

Nisibis is, therefore, like Pomerius' establishment in Arles, an intermediate state: halfway from the philosophical schools of Athens and Alexandria to monastic centres and their libraries. The school was inside the city but also a bit of a city of its own, with a social separation, its own baths, and its own rules. The roots of this practice might have to do with the influence of rabbinic centres, and it continued under the Abbasid caliphate.[209] This is then not a simple linear evolution but rather one of the branch outs of monasticism. In this branch, urban schools of rhetoric coexisted and mingled with quasi-monastic educational institutions for monks and laypeople. Under a theological hardening used as a function of distinction, they become models for monasteries. This hardening in the case of Nisibis led to its demise – a group of around 600 students adhering to stricter theological argumentation and a limit to free exegesis refounded the school as a monastery outside of the city.[210] The school, as it was known before, stops being referenced afterwards. But even its successor, the monastery of Abraham of Kashkar (d. 586), does not leave the spiritual suburbs of the city of Nisibis.[211]

The examples of Nisibis and the school of Pomerius show that there can be no clear-cut distinction between urban secular and 'monastic' Christian learning. Even if both sides polemicised against each other, one must see this as a rhetorical strategy of distinction. On the ground, the differences could be marginal, and both 'sides' profited from shared examples and a shared community of students. The differences between such establishments like the school of Pomerius and a monastery were fuzzy enough to allow both to be seen as compatible. Nisibis and Arles are also more similar than we think at first glance: both are quasi-monastic institutions in a city, run by someone who, in the eyes of

---

[204] See *The Statutes of the School of Nisibis*, canon 5.

[205] *Historia Monachorum in Aegypto*, ch. 18 (Sarapion).

[206] Iso'yahb III, *Letters*, part 3, nr. 10.

[207] See chapter 'Monasticism as an Afroeurasian Phenomenon'.

[208] *The Statutes of the School of Nisibis.*   [209] Becker 2006, pp. 3, 135.   [210] Reinink 1995.

[211] Camplani 2007, pp. 281–2.

his contemporaries, was an 'abbot', and their pupils could be considered monks. As the example of Caesarius shows, they were also frequented by active monks who could come and go.

Those side branches of late antique and early medieval monasticism did not become extinct but were incorporated into more distinctive forms. They also left durable traces in the more successful variations of the phenomenon. Their genetic code is discernible both in immediate successors like Caesarius or Abraham of Kashkar, and the writings they have produced were read centuries after those forms had died out. Their gene of learning made monasticism more robust but also more versatile.

This influence of the intermediate forms of monasticism only strengthened the expectation of education that we have encountered at the beginning. The nuns in Caesarius' rule for virgins were expected to read for two hours a day. There is no biblical or ascetic reasoning for it, but the school heritage can provide an explanation. Pomerius supposedly also wrote a rule for virgins.[212] We will never know what provisions he included in it, but maybe in the words of his pupil, Caesarius, we are hearing an echo of the views of his teacher. This shows us that not only urban schools influenced monastic rules but also that this transfer, at least in the realities of the fifth and early sixth century, happened in the urban milieu.

We must not think of those monastic or quasi-monastic schools as a replacement or a simple direct continuation of *paideia*. They are a parallel, equivalent phenomenon, running for some time alongside other forms of civic education. That the School of Nisibis was seen by its contemporaries as an equivalent of urban teaching or at least very much resembling it is also confirmed by the preface to Junillus's *Instituta Regularia*, where he writes in mid-sixth-century Constantinople about Paul the Persian that he 'was educated at the Syrian School in the city of Nisibis, where the Divine Law is taught in a disciplined and orderly fashion by public teachers in the same way in a secular education grammar and rhetoric are taught among us [in the cities]'.[213] All the essential features seem to have been fulfilled here: the teachers were 'public', there was a curriculum which ensured 'a disciplined and orderly fashion', and the form of teaching was the same as in the cities. Nisibis and the whole Syriac school movement were not only intertwined with monasticism but also seen as a form of it.[214] These were connected, parallel movements that fed each other and sometimes were indistinguishable, even if at times they found themselves in conflict. Their connections to urban space were often similar.

---

[212] Leyser 2000, p. 67.   [213] Maas 2003, pp. 119–21.   [214] Becker 2006, p. 172.

Monastic Education with and without the City

We have already seen that those establishments can be spotted across the Broad Mediterranean, but they are also connected. Cassiodorus in Italy was fascinated by Nisibis as an idea, even if he did not know any precise details about it. His knowledge was filtered through the urban milieu of Constantinople and the work of Junillus.[215] Nisibis was attractive enough to consider it as a model for Cassiodorus' city-university planned together with pope Agapetus. The failure of this project was not due to the cities being too urban, too distracting, and too spiritually dangerous to run such an institution within them. It was rather due to cities failing at what they were supposed to do in the first place.

As Cassiodorus made clear, the cities became too insecure in Italy; the wars of the sixth century made them unsuited for a Western version of Nisibis. Monastic learning needed to go elsewhere (see Figure 10). But we should not interpret this move to the countryside as an antagonism to the city. Instead, it highlights once more the fragility of urbanism in Late Antiquity which prevented the cities (surely temporarily, according to Cassiodorus) from fulfilling their educational functions. At the same time, the choice of the countryside has a lot to do with Cassiodorus' personal decisions and his retirement from politics.[216] Monasticism's rhetoric of the search for the desert was a more than welcome distraction from a possibly pragmatic decision.

Cassiodorus is fascinated both by the idea of an institution dedicated to learning and the ideal of educated *cives*. He cannot realise both simultaneously, but he still tries to fuse both concepts in a monastery. He gives us his 'precise' models for his plan: the schools of Alexandria and Nisibis. Alexandria had a problematic doctrinal relationship to Rome and Constantinople, to say the least. Nisibis, on the other hand, might seem strange at first glance. Not only is this school in the Persian Empire, but Cassiodorus bizarrely claims that the school is run by and for Jews. The literarisation of the movement shows itself: the precise lineage was necessary as long as it fulfilled the rules that monasticism as a genre prescribed. By taking Alexandria and Nisibis as examples, Cassiodorus was, paradoxically, making his institution less controversial.

Cassiodorus did not limit himself to promoting city academies as an example for monasteries. He also paid special attention to the activity of copying books. In the late Roman context, this was an urban pursuit – the necessary education, resources, and clientele were concentrated in cities.[217] As we have seen at the beginning of this Element, for Jerome in the desert of Chalcis, it was necessary to bring a team of scribes and students to keep up the scribal activity. But this

---

[215] Pollheimer 2015, p. 120.   [216] Vanderspoel 1990.
[217] Hose 2019 for the link between education and the city in antiquity.

Figure 10 Cassiodorus envisaged Vivarium as a better city. We do not know how the monastery actually looked, but this is how a late eighth-century illuminator envisaged it – including a fishpond. Bamberg Msc.Patr. 61, fol. 29v. Photo: Gerald Raab / Staatsbibliothek Bamberg

proto-scriptorium was not yet an approved monastic practice. It was but a transplant of an urban activity into the 'literary desert'. For Cassiodorus, Jerome's emphasis on copying and correcting books was an important model. But the true innovation he brought was the institutionalisation of this pursuit as a necessary monastic practice. If monasteries were to survive in the age of weakening urban systems and crisis, they had to create an environment where it was possible to continue urban pursuits like copying books. The monastery fulfilled urban functions that the cities could not guarantee anymore. Moreover, for Cassiodorus and his monks, the monastery did it better. 'You have received a kind of city of your own, pious citizens', he promised his monks.[218]

This process of convergence gained momentum in the second half of the sixth century. Only a few years after Cassiodorus, Gregory the Great pursued his spiritual and educational goals similarly. He turned his family's *villa suburbana*, on Caelio close to the Circus Maximus, into an exclusive monastery that was supposed to strengthen his network and to produce both an impressive library and a place of learning. He did not forget to include lavish portraits of himself and his parents on its walls in the process.[219] It is difficult to say why he deemed Rome a suitable place for this institution when, twenty years earlier, Cassiodorus had shied away from staying in a large city. It could come down to a more secure and politically stable situation in central Italy, but also to specific interests of both actors. Maybe Gregory wanted to strengthen his influence on Rome's urban elite networks and was bound to Rome anyway. Cassiodorus might have considered his political ambitions over and chose to abstain from potentially disruptive local politics.

Gregory's establishment paid equal attention to the pursuits that were important to Cassiodorus and to Benedict, including a focus on learning. A close look at his over 200 letters concerned with matters of monastic discipline and organisation shows that he remained a pragmatic interpreter of tradition.[220] His monastery became a school for the missionary clergy and monks; in many ways, it is the place where the idea of the Christian mission in the West was developed. The cadre of the mission to Britain in the 590s was educated here. St Andrew's monastery, a former urban villa of Gregory's family, produced books as well. It is possible that Augustine of Canterbury (d. 604) took manuscripts with him to Britain which were connected to or produced in Gregory's 'laboratory'. Canterbury itself, with a monastery in the spiritual suburbs of a former Roman city, became an important centre of learning and copying books. Bede muses how in the late seventh century monks in Canterbury could use Latin and Greek like native speakers, due to the influence of bishop (and former monk) Theodore (602–690), who came from Tarsus in Asia Minor, and abbot Hadrian (d. 710) from North Africa.[221] The networks of the Broad Mediterranean were still very much active, and monasteries were slowly playing the same role in them as cities did.

---

[218] Cassiodorus, *Institutions*, book 1, c. 15, 30, 3.   [219] Meyvaert 1994, pp. 3–5.
[220] Markus 1997, pp. 68–72.
[221] Bede, *Ecclesiastical History of the English People*, book 4, c. 2.

In the late seventh century, in the territory of Astorga, an urban centre in Leon, an extraordinary monastic writer was active. Valerius of Bierzo (d. c. 695), who came from the Visigothic elite, was well-educated and left a rich body of work. In his twenties, he decided to pursue a monastic life but could not see himself fitting in with any existing monastic institution. Instead, he ostensibly opted for an ascetic life in the mountains. He never left the immediate vicinity of Astorga, and his hermitages were located on estates near public roads.[222] He maintained access to a rich library that included the works of Jerome, Athanasius, and Isidore, which seems to have fallen victim to book robbers more than once.[223] He also practised a form of autobiographical confessional literature and left as many as three such texts.[224] Cities and their territories geographically delineate his world.[225] They offer us an unprecedented insight into how he wanted to project his ascetic persona onto a literary public sphere. His autobiographies maintain direct links to the *Life of Anthony* and are therefore poignant examples of monastic identity as a literary genre. In many ways, they also betray how well informed Valerius was about the world he professed to abscond.[226]

Valerius' life was full of the apparent tension between the life of the holy hermit and the pressure for increased institutionalisation. He fought with his patrons who wanted him to become a priest, and bishops who tried to entice him to come back to the city.[227] He instructed monks and stylised himself as the last man standing of the true, desert-driven asceticism. We might even conjecture that he enjoyed the constant attention.[228] The crucial element is another part of his persona: that of a teacher, an involved pedagogue, keen on developing or perfecting various learning techniques. He taught boys how to read and write, boasting that his divinely inspired methods allowed them to master all psalms in six months. After instructing a well-off young boy in letters, he gave him a book, a gift written especially for the boy. This literary guide to life is symptomatic of Valerius' understanding of education. We do not have any proof but this text could have been a version of his *De vana saeculi sapientia*, his tractate on ascetic living in the secular world. Simply put, he ran a school and received pupils. He was, for all purposes, an ascetic version of a rhetor. One cannot help but think of Nisibis and Pomerius (and Libanius for that matter)

---

[222] Martin 2017–18, pp. 62, 65.

[223] Those get stolen from him by a priest Flaino, see Valerius of Bierzo, *Ordo Querimoniae*, c. 3. Valerius loudly complains about all the books he had lost from his 'hermitage'. He also refers to the process of gathering a library in other places, for example, his *Residuum*, c. 2.

[224] Collins 1992.   [225] Valerius of Bierzo, *Ordo Querimoniae*, c. 1.

[226] Valverde Castro 2011.   [227] Valerius of Bierzo, *Ordo Querimoniae*, c. 7.

[228] Diniz 2021, pp. 153–7.

when Valerius describes how his disciples came for the summer and left him in the winter.[229]

This is a time when monasteries start to play an important role in education, but also a time when they begin to change. Maybe the time was up for self-professed ascetics and freelance teachers. Under the influence of such writers like Isidore of Seville (d. 636) or Fructuosus of Braga (d. 665), organised and institutionalised monasteries gained the upper hand in education. Clerical authorities organised monastic space in such a way as to facilitate teaching and spiritual formation.[230] It is not only about being separate from 'the world' (while, lest we forget, being in practice intertwined with it). Now the monastic space needed its own spatial hierarchy to fulfil its educational functions. Cities had had spaces for education and now monasteries developed their own. In this world, Valerius, a highly educated ascetic freelancer, had understandably met with pushback. His struggles to get to the desert remind us of Jerome, whom he read, and for whom chasing that topos was in no way contradictory to making full use of his urban education and socialisation. Valerius was closer to Didymus or Pomerius than to the monastic world of Isidore's rule. Still, in the late seventh century, if you wanted to partake in monasticism, an urban education and rhetorical practices gave you a front-row seat. Valerius' world, rarely more than a day's journey from a city, and full of books and literary allusions, is a perfect spiritual suburb. But increasingly, there is a change in the air; monasteries can now do what the cities cannot. The epoch of parallel development draws to a close.

***

In 679–680, Ceolfrith, prior of Wearmouth-Jarrow in Northumbria, like the good monk that he was, travelled to Rome to get some books. He acquired the so-called *Codex Grandior*, a massive Bible produced in Vivarium under the direct supervision of Cassiodorus.[231] The codex is lost to us, but a copy made in Northumbria and derived from it survives: the *Codex Amiatinus* (made of circa 515 dead animals). On folio 5r, there is a full-page miniature of the prophet Ezra, copying a book in front of a cupboard filled with nine volumes of the Bible. In a twist of fate this image was once Cassiodorus himself, reinterpreted as Ezra by the monks of Wearmouth-Jarrow. But this thread of monastic tradition is not all: the *Codex Amiatinus* shows how monks from the periphery of the Broad Mediterranean would now use their connections and substantial resources to go to cities to look for books. They saw themselves in the same literary community as their predecessors in Italy and beyond. Moreover, the monasteries had become so rich that

---

[229] Valerius of Bierzo, *Replicatio*, c. 6, 2, 4.　　[230] Wood 2017.　　[231] Meyvaert 1996, p. 836.

they could go back to Rome and present the codex as a gift to the pope. Ceolfrith set out to Rome in 716 with the richly decorated book. He died on the way in Burgundy and the book never made it to its destination. Monasteries, in the spirit of the pupil that became the master, were now rich centres of education that connected the Broad Mediterranean.

5 Monasticism as an Afroeurasian Phenomenon

From India, from Persia, from Ethiopia we daily welcome monks in crowds. The Armenian bowman has laid aside his quiver, the Huns learn the psalter, the chilly Scythians are warmed with the glow of the faith.

Jerome, Ep. 107

While we have now seen various interactions between monasticism and cities in the core of the Broad Mediterranean region, we also need to look at its extremities, both geographical and chronological. Monasticism had quickly become a widespread movement. As Jerome wrote in 403 in the quote just mentioned, monasticism was already an Afroeurasian genre. Let us then follow Jerome's example and look above and beyond. Christian monks in Persia, China, or Ireland and under Muslim rule have not stopped interacting with the urban space.

In 554, the clerics at the synod of Mar Joseph had a problem to solve. The Mar Acacius synod in 486 had forbidden building monasteries and any forms of monasticism within the city limits.[232] The synod's motivation was complex. On the one hand, it had to do with the trappings of pastoral care in a difficult religious terrain of Sasanian Persia; bishops were simply afraid to lose their flock to monks. At the same time the synod of 486 was dealing with an underlying feeling of unease with core tenets of monasticism: celibacy was seen as unnatural and as contrary to Persian society's requirement of producing offspring. The synod fathers did not, however, see a fundamental contradiction between urban and monastic milieus. No matter what their concerns were, at the end the prohibition backfired. Monks did not suddenly disappear from Persian cities but 'pagans and Jews' rejoiced that, through the lack of organised monasteries, Christianity was on the back foot in urban spaces. The learned fathers of the synod of 554 decided to counteract and 'according to the tradition and habit that exists in the holy church since the times of blessed apostles to this day', they wished that 'churches, monasteries, temples, and martyria be built inside cities and in their vicinity'.[233] Monks were still forbidden to liturgically compete with bishops' churches, but their position was now secure. The monks were back on the block.

---

[232] The Synod of Mar Acacius, canon 2.   [233] The Synod of Mar Joseph, canon 20.

This was a major shift for the church of the East, but we should also interpret the decision as the institutional acceptance of an existing practice and as readiness to reap the benefits of urban monasticism. This decision did not come out of the blue. Apparently, it was due to the influence of Mar Aba (d. 552), a member of the Sasanian elite and an alumnus of both the School of Nisibis and the School of Alexandria. Mar Aba was a fascinating figure. He travelled around the Roman Empire, visited Athens and other cities.[234] Fuelled by this experience, he put in motion a large reform programme.[235] Part of that programme was a change of attitude towards monasticism and the presence of monks in the urban space of Persia. The know-how gathered throughout the Broad Mediterranean influenced various forms of monastic and urban coexistence outside of its immediate borders.

Monastic presence inside the cities of the Sasanian Empire was not only a matter of settling differences within the church. It was also a question of sealing a long-term manifestation of Christianity within the urban tissue of the empire. Sasanian Persia possessed a rich urban landscape.[236] In this landscape it was only to be expected to encounter urban monasteries. Enshrining the decision to allow them in cities on a synodal level, as it happened in 554, was proof of the growing acceptance of Christian monasticism in Persian society.[237] Reservations towards monasticism's habitus, and the subject of celibacy, had to be brushed aside. This tells us a lot about the importance attached to monastic presence in cities – a calling card, if you will, of eastern Christianity.[238]

But since it was about prestige, it was also about patronage. Khosrow II patronised monasteries in Jerusalem during the Persian conquest.[239] Sasanian rulers sponsored monasteries in their cities and in their immediate vicinity.[240] It was only logical that both sides would want to benefit from urban exposure of monasticism. For the Sasanian elite, monasteries apparently offered an alternative to a secular career – just as they did in the Mediterranean West. In late Sasanian and early Islamic Mesopotamia we find abundant traces of aristocratic families focusing their fortunes and their fame on monasteries. In the Book of Chastity, an eighth-century bishop of Basrah in today's Iraq, Iso'dnaḥ described several monastic founders who belonged to the Persian aristocracy and the urban elite. There we meet Mar Job, a child of rich merchants who himself traded in pearls with the Roman Empire. He was educated at Nisibis and

---

[234] Payne 2015, pp. 95–6.   [235] Izdebski 2019, pp. 187–8.   [236] Simpson 2017.
[237] Wood 2013, p. 148.
[238] This is not uncommon: we have reason to believe that monasteries at the approaches to Nubian cities served as a form of 'advertisement' that the settlement was Christian, see Obłuski 2019, p. 141.
[239] Payne 2015, p. 183.   [240] Canepa 2018, pp. 140, 143.

eventually decided to found a monastery. We also meet founders like Mar John or George who belonged to the Sasanian royal family.[241] One can interpret these instances as examples of the Persian aristocracy substituting their access to lay and state offices. After the Muslim conquest, investments into monasticism might have been seen as a way of securing influence and property in times of political readjustments, continuing the flow between urban and monastic environments.[242]

As catholicos Iso'yahb III wrote in the 650s, new Muslim rulers allowed business as usual for monasteries and churches. Not only did they not attack the Christian churches, they also supported them with gifts and respected their institutions.[243] Even if we take this with a grain of salt, it seems that the established social practice of patronising monasteries and churches was continued by the new rulers.[244] Take the case of John of Dailam (d. 738), a wandering monk who founded several monasteries late in his life. The transmission of his *vita* shows his widespread renown: Thomas, the ninth-century bishop of Marga, noted that his own account of John's life was held rather short because so many other detailed versions had already been written. Translations appear throughout the Broad Mediterranean, including Arab and Ge'ez versions (with extant Sogdian fragments). His Syriac life exists in both prose and verse.[245]

John was born in Hdatta on the river Tigris, an important city with a bishopric in the seventh and eighth centuries. John learned about monasticism from monks (from Beth Abe, one of the biggest and most influential monasteries of the region) who frequented his parents' city house. As a consequence, he turned towards a monastic life. His early career was dramatic: he was taken captive in a military conflict and was sold as a slave to the shores of the Caspian Sea. After cursing (and thereby killing) his owner and all nine of the man's children, and after surviving the penalty of being burned alive, he roamed free in the region and converted many people. Afterwards, his monastic vocation turned thoroughly urban: he visited the caliph in Damascus and attained (through another wonder) the right to found monasteries wherever he wanted. After healing the caliph's governor of Iraq, Al-Hajjaj Ibn Yusuf, he settled on a mountain near the city of Arrajan. This originally Sasanian foundation was a vital hub for commerce between Fars, Khuzestan, and merchants from the Persian Gulf.[246] Here, John founded a monastery for a mixed community of Syriac and Persian-speaking monks. After quarrels between the two factions, and a sign from

---

[241] Iso'dnah, *The Book of Chastity*, c. 9, 11, 12, 17, 36, 86, 88, 112, 44, 7, 21.
[242] Morony 1974, pp. 126–7.   [243] Iso'yahb III, *Letters*, part 3, nr. 14; see Ioan 2009, p. 99.
[244] Tannous 2018, p. 381.   [245] Brock 1981–2.   [246] Gaube 1986.

God, he founded a second monastery on the other side of the valley to separate the factions.[247]

John of Dailam's case shows that the keys to a successful monastery remained twofold. On the one hand, a monk had to reach a degree of fame that allowed him access to important figures who provided land and money. On the other, he had to get either into a city or close to it, where pilgrims, goods, and influence were waiting to fill the monastery with life and prosperity. From John's story we can conjecture that the Muslim rulers did not see Christian monastic communities in the early medieval Middle East as incompatible with their view of the social landscape. Quite the contrary: those rulers were often sought out as patrons, and as useful addressees when it came to avoiding paying taxes. Monasteries from the times of Sabas to John of Dailam continued to view themselves as corporate bodies in correspondence with secular rule, no matter whether their ruler was orthodox, heterodox, Zoroastrian, or Muslim.

What is missing from the story of John of Dailam is the status of monastic education in those changed circumstances. Fortunately, such figures as Jacob of Edessa (d. 708) provide us with examples of continuity in this area. Jacob was born in Antioch in the middle of the seventh century, a contemporary of John. He spent his life between cities, monasteries, and schools. He supposedly studied in Alexandria and wrote extensively on such topics as canon law, philosophy, grammar, and history. He corresponded widely with other scholars in the region. As a monk, he was elected to be the bishop of Edessa but stepped down to pursue a strict monastic life. This pursuit led him to a convent in Antioch. There he taught, continuing the tradition of monastic education. He supposedly returned to the bishop's seat just before dying of old age.[248]

Muslim writers emphasised that caliphs were active in giving out money and other support for the construction of churches and monasteries. Monasteries continued to produce books, oil, and wine under new political circumstances. Those were goods difficult to get. Knowledge, especially of pre-Islamic history, was vital for many. So was getting your hands on a good amphora of wine, restricted for Muslims, yet connected to monastic production and needed at the very least for the Eucharist.[249] All that was secured through the patronage and support of monasteries. Those monasteries remained integrated into urban economies and hinterlands.

All in all, it was then business as usual under Muslim rule, as far as the circumstances allowed. In fact, a close analysis of large urban spaces under Islam, like Edessa, shows that old monasteries still thrived in Late Antiquity and

---

[247] *Life of John of Dailam*, ch. 40.   [248] Salvesen 2008.

[249] Tannous 2018, pp. 381–6, 461–73.

the Early Middle Ages and new ones continued to be built. It is not until the tenth century that they began to disappear or at least lose their prominence in the urban landscape.[250] It comes then as no surprise that when Christians reached Tang China, a highly bureaucratised state with a rich urban landscape; it is to the cities that they turned to found monasteries.

A look over to China might surprise us here – it cannot, even by a stretch, be seen as part of the Mediterranean world. But the spread of eastern Christianity first through Central Asia and then the western fringes of the Tang sphere of influence shows that texts, views, and ideas about monasticism were widely received and that those worlds were connected. In Central Asia, the identification of Christian sites as monasteries remains difficult. Churches in places like Ak-Beshim in Kyrgyzstan confirm Christian presence in towns but cannot indisputably be identified as monasteries.[251] We need to go further east for solid evidence. The finds in the monastery of Bulayïq, situated in the immediate vicinity of the cities of Turfan and Gaochang in modern Xinjang included hundreds of Sogdian, Syriac, and Uighur texts and translations, among them fragments of the *Apophthegmata Patrum*, works of Evagrius and a version of the Life of John of Dailam.[252] Some of the texts in the monastery, dating to the late eighth and early ninth centuries, show that the monks there were well informed about what was happening in Seleucia-Ctesiphon, providing them with a direct link to the heart of the Syriac Christianity.[253]

When we then look at sources from Tang China proper, we see that this connection remains. The Xi'an stele, erected in Chang'an in 781 with inscriptions both in Syriac and Chinese characters, not only mentions the patriarch of the East residing in Seleucia-Ctesiphon but most importantly it describes how Christianity was brought to China by 'Alopen' and how the first monastery, the Da Qin Monastery, was established in 638 in the imperial capital.[254] The stele informs us that emperor Gaozong (650–683) patronised an establishment of a monastery in every prefecture – and indeed in 2006 another stele was found, this time in Luoyang, the second capital of the Tang, dating from 815.[255] The second stele shows a complex ecclesiastical and monastic organisation, based on Syriac examples but expressed in Buddhist vocabulary, in the middle of a teeming metropolis,[256] a year after Charlemagne's death. These connections, or rather the common framework of expressing monastic presence in the city, do make us pause. Monks and nuns continued to flock to cities. When monks from Palestine fled Persian and Arab invasions in the first half of the seventh century, they settled in Rome, in a former city *domus*, and played

---

[250] Guidetti 2009.   [251] Klein 2004.   [252] Hunter 2012.   [253] Hunter 2021.
[254] Barat 2002.   [255] Nicolini-Zani 2009.   [256] Nicolini-Zani 2013.

a crucial role in the Lateran synod of 649.[257] Their monastery became a power centre of early medieval Rome.[258] The communities of St Sabas in Rome and the 'Nestorian' monastery in Chang'an might have never known about each other but they all existed in the same monastic genre.

In Faras (ancient Pachoras), the capital of Nobatia and later part of Makuria, prosperous Nubian kingdoms placed strategically between Islamic Egypt and Ethiopia, salvage excavations in the 1960s have uncovered an extensive palatial-ecclesiastical complex in the middle of a town, best known for the stunning frescoes from the cathedral. The complex included a monastery, right next to townhouses literally propped against the walls of the monastic church.[259] There were many monasteries associated with cities in Nubia, mostly in the spiritual suburbs. Nevertheless, it is in the anchoretic tradition that we find the most striking examples of monastic integration into the city. Most Nubian hermitages were located above cities or settlements and directed towards them.[260] Not only could the anchorite see the city every time they went out of their cave, but the inhabitants of the town could also observe monastic life above them. Further south, in Ethiopia, we see that the integration of monasticism and urban space had a lot in common with this practice. In its earliest form in the Aksumite period, Ethiopian monasticism was inspired by Syrian and Egyptian examples. The archaeological record seems to show that the separation from urban contexts was taken seriously. But an analysis of the traces of early monastic establishment in the actual landscape shows that what was important was again a *vertical* separation. The cells of abbas Pantaleon and Likanos (said to have come from Rome and Constantinople in the hagiographical tradition) were built high above the capital of the empire, Aksum.[261] You could not only see the city from them, but you could see *them* from many places in the city. Apart and yet inescapable, with an urban connection carefully preserved in the written record.

Nevertheless, a separation or at least a distance is recognisable, even if the founding fathers seemed to have a particular penchant for urban space. What to do though if there are no cities to work with? You become one, at least on paper. In Ireland, on the opposite end of Eurasia, Christianity owed its success to monastic efforts. But Ireland did not have cities, at least not in the sense that we can apply in the Roman Empire or China or Ethiopia for that matter. This led to a peculiar situation where the Irish church had both mighty abbots and a complete episcopal organisation where the bishops ruled over a *tuath*, a territory of a petty kingdom.[262] Monasteries were referred to in written

---

[257] *The Acts of the Lateran Synod of 649*, pp. 136–7.   [258] Patrich 2001, p. 13.

[259] Michałowski 1967, p. 67.   [260] Obłuski 2019, pp. 140–4.   [261] Finneran 2012.

[262] Charles-Edwards 2000, p. 259.

sources as *civitates*, where authors tried to find the nearest category they could use to express what they knew.[263] This pre-eminence of monasteries in ecclesiastical organisation and in the economic tissue of the island has led to an emergence of the monastic town framework in research, in which the monastery by the ninth century for all purposes *was* a city in early medieval Ireland.[264] The monasteries of early medieval Ireland, like Clonmacnoise, masqueraded as cities so well that they convinced some scholars in the twentieth century. But a close look at the evidence shows that the situation was much more complicated. While monasteries in Ireland did attract lay population and in some cases were centres of trade and craftsmanship, they were not exactly towns.[265] While the language used, including naming the zones outside the core of monastic settlement as *suburbana*, was deceptively urban and civic, the roots of its use were not connected with cities but with religious use.[266] In order to remain within the genre, monasticism and monastic literature had co-opted this vocabulary and the city.

Here, on the shores of the Atlantic Ocean sometime in the ninth century, this Element comes to an end. It is a paradoxical place to finish, in a land without cities, on the periphery of the Broad Mediterranean world, after a monastic whistle-stop tour of Afroeurasia. But beyond the ninth century a different, although connected, world awaits: indebted to the understanding of monasticism as ever linked to the city but looking for its own solutions, where sometimes it was the towns that landed in the spiritual suburbs of monasteries.[267] In this last section, we had a chance to see how the relationship between monasticism and the city looked above and beyond the Broad Mediterranean and the span of Late Antiquity. Many places, like Georgia or Armenia, we did not have time or space to visit. But the traces that we have seen only support the view that this relationship was an extremely strong one.

Conclusions

The credits do not really roll on this story. All the major characters that we met, Mary and Jerome, Anthony and Columbanus, Melania and Paula, Caesarius and Rabbula, continued to play their part in monasticism – even after death. Their writings and lives continued to impact this genre of society well beyond the first millennium and beyond the Broad Mediterranean. Their legacy would prove to be a backbone to the epoch that we now call the Middle Ages.

One of the key reasons for this success was a mechanism we have called literarisation: the process of converting ascetic practice into literature and the

---

[263] Etchingham 2002, p. 457.   [264] Doherty 1985.   [265] Ó Carragáin 2015.
[266] Swift 1998, pp. 105–25.   [267] McKitterick 1979.

subsequent shaping of social reality through this literature. Literarisation makes our metaphor of monasticism as a genre so enticing. The norms of monasticism functioned analogously to the rules of literary genres and they also naturally evolved over time. Literarisation allowed for three ways of integration into monasticism. You could either be written into the genre by someone else (as in the case of Mary of Egypt), you could actively write yourself into it (as did Jerome), or you could emulate the prescriptions of existing monastic literature. All three ways were open to interpretation, and thus flexible in a changing frame of expectations – expectations that were under the constant influence of cities. The entanglement of monastic archetypes and their historical *personae* was normal (see Figure 11). We can see it everywhere, it is in Hilarion as well as in Martin of Tours or Mary of Egypt. Some of them were real people others were not. Their stories were valid nonetheless.

The close connection of monasticism with urbanism is traceable from the very beginning. It produced a tension that became the catalyst for the literarisation of the whole movement. From Anthony and Pachomius on, eremites and monastic communities never lost their connection to the city. Moreover, monasteries began to resemble towns themselves: be it in their legal position or their corporate identity, groups of monks and nuns and monasteries behaved like cities, and were treated as cities by other institutions. Throughout the Broad Mediterranean, they started to take over some of the functions of cities as well. In providing organisation to productive rural spaces or in providing a stage for aristocratic wealth and power, monastic communities quickly became viable alternatives. This alternative was also decidedly more attractive to Christian audiences: monasteries were better, more heavenly cities, here on earth. With time came in many regions the relocation of cultural hegemony from cities to monasteries, a *translatio* of forms and functions.

But the relationship of monasticism and the city also had a more mundane facet: nuns and monks were a common sight on the streets of late antique and early medieval towns. Because of the diversity of ascetic practices, many communities either lived in town houses or were, like the nuns of Caesarius of Arles, consciously placed in the urban space. This has often caused friction, sometimes making monastics a significant political force in the East and an unruly group in the West. The urban populace remained a key audience of monasticism as well. Members of that audience were prime candidates for joining the monastic genre of society; and educated, affluent urbanites ranked among the most prominent protagonists of the movement. The preoccupation of many monastic texts with typically urban concerns comes then as no surprise.

While numerous texts highlight the presumed illiteracy of their heroes, many of them tended to be able to read and write: even Mary of Egypt left a note in the

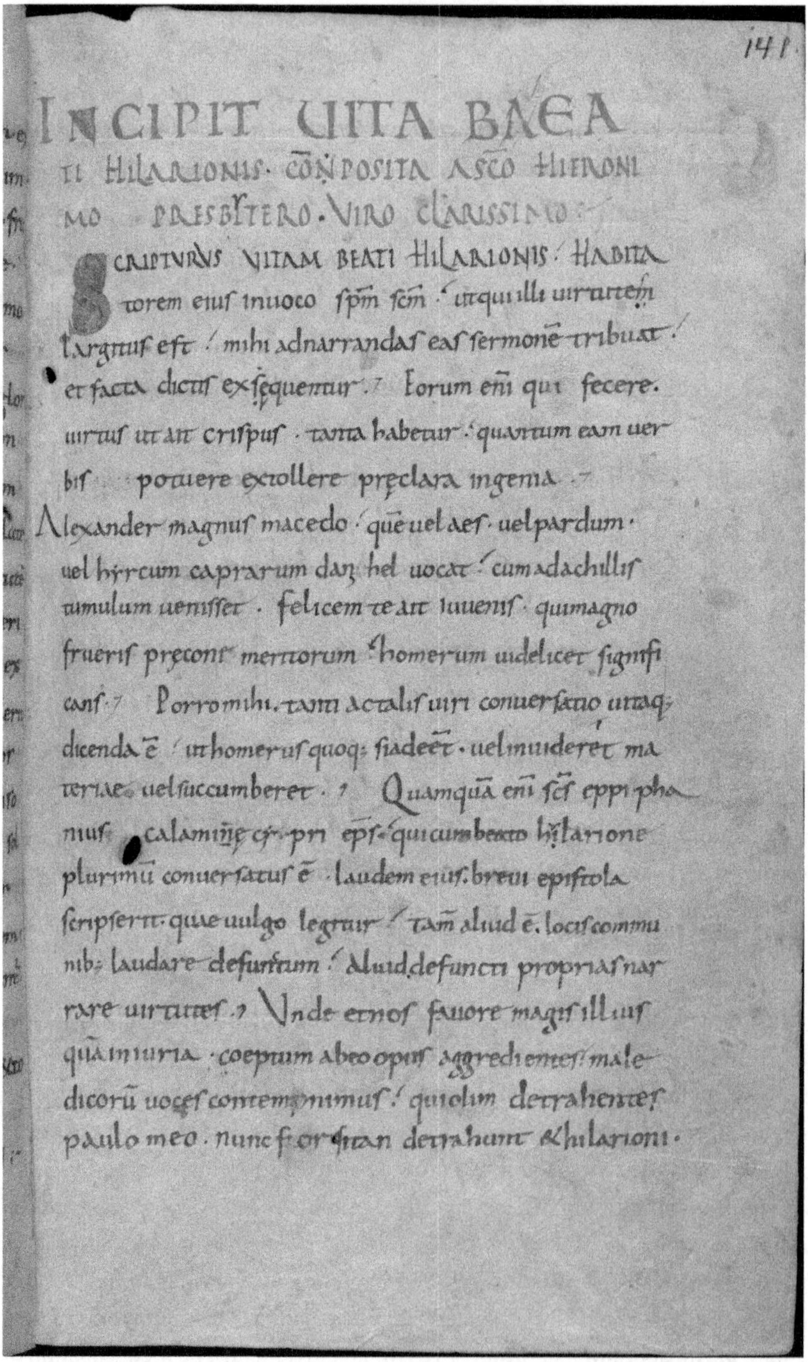

INCIPIT UITA BÆA
TI Hilarionis· Composita a sco Hieroni
mo presbitero·Uiro clarissimo

Scripturus uitam beati Hilarionis· Habita
torem eius inuoco spm scm· utquiilli uirrutem
largirius est / mihi adnarrandas eas sermone tribuat·
et facta dictis exsequentur·/ Eorum eni qui fecere·
uirtus ut ait crispus· tanta habetur· quantum eam uer
bis potuere extollere preclara ingenia·/
Alexander magnus macedo· que uel aes· uelpardum·
uel hyrcum caprarum dar hel uocat· cumadachillis
tumulum uenisset· felicem te ait luuenis· quimagno
frueris preconis meritorum homerum uidelicet signifi
cans·/ Porromihi· tanti actalis uiri conuersatio utraq;
dicenda e / uthomerus quoq; siadeet· uelinuideret ma
teriae· uelsuccumberet·/ Quamquam eni scs eppi pha
nius· calaminae cr· pri eps· quicumbeato hilarione
plurimu conuersatus e· laudem eius· breui epistola
scripserit· quae uulgo legitur / tam aliud e· locis commu
nibz laudare defunctum· Aliuddefuncti proprias nar
rare uirtutes·/ Unde etnos fauore magisilluis
quam iniuria· coeptum abeo opus aggredientes male
dicorum uoces contemnimus / quiolim detrahentes
paulo meo· nunc fr· orsitan detrahant & hilarioni·

Figure 11 Here, in a composite manuscript of the early ninth century, they all meet: Antonius, Athanasius, Jerome, Hilarion, Caesarius, and John Chrysostom. St Gallen, Stiftsbibliothek, Cod. Sang. 558: Composite manuscript, p. 141 and 193 © Stiftsbibliothek St Gallen

INDI NOMINE INCIPIVNT

OMELIAE SCI CESARII EPISCOPI ARELATEH

NUMERO DUODECIM

nter reliquas beatitudines quas in
euangelio dns & saluator noster enu
merare dignatus est, etia hoc addi
dit dicens; Beati qui esuriunt & sitiunt
iustitia, quo ipsi saturabuntur; Feli
ces sunt quibus istam p̄ claram famem
& desiderabilem sitim dr̄ donare dig
natur; quomodo aut esuritur iustitia
frs̄ iustitiam esuris; siuerbum dī pa
tienter & libenter audire volueris;
De tali eni cibo dictum est; qui edunt
me adhuc esuriunt, & qui bibunt me
adhuc sitiunt; quam uis eni melius sit
facere quam nosse, prius tamen est nos
se quā facere; Deb& eni discere quae op
tet implere; Denique audi scripturā
dicentem; Omnis qui non didicerit ius
titiam sup terram, ueritatem non fa
ciet; Et iterum; zelus adprehendit
populum ineruditum, & ignis aduer

sand, and Anthony wrote letters to his flock. Books, letters, and notes are commonplace in monastic stories because monasticism, driven by literarisation, had a vital interest in education. Authors of rules expected monks and nuns to be able to read or listen to prescribed reading aloud. Part of the appeal of monasticism was this inherent formative aspect: monasticism promised access to learning. The city was simply necessary for the development of this important tenet: intermediate phenomena like the School of Nisibis or the School of Pomerius built a bridge between the worlds of urbanism and monasticism. Theirs was not an easy relationship but it shaped the movement for centuries to come.

On these pages, our goal was to show how monasticism thrived in the shadow of the late antique city. There certainly was a degree of reciprocity. At some point monasteries and the legacy of the movement started to uphold the urban landscape. They became necessary for both the spiritual and worldly economies of towns. Caesarius' Arles, Gregory's Rome, or Rabbula's Edessa were all heavily influenced by monasticism. This productive tension between monastics and urban space is a central feature in the Broad Mediterranean, but it is also visible beyond it. Christian monasteries made their way into cities in Ethiopia, Persia, or China. Their presence shows the ability to flourish in diverse societies, geographically distant from where it originally developed. Key texts like the Life of John of Dailam or the Life of Mary of Egypt were effectively Afroeurasian connectors.

City and monasticism were never truly opposites. It is difficult to imagine late antique and early medieval monasticism without the city. As a genre of society it owed much to urbanism: its educational and its distributional capabilities, its resources and its supportive audiences. Even in praising the desert, monasticism lived through the city.

Appendix

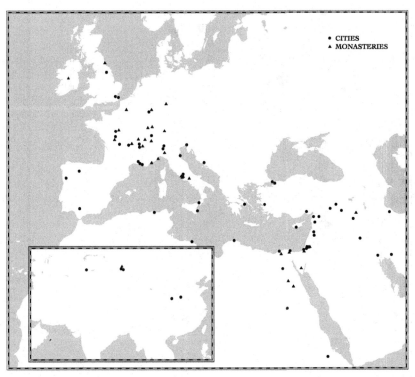

Map 1 Places mentioned in the text. Drawn by Lukasz P. Fafinski

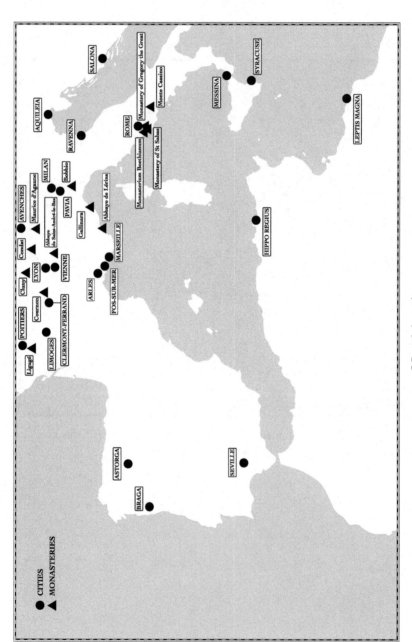

Map 1 (cont.)

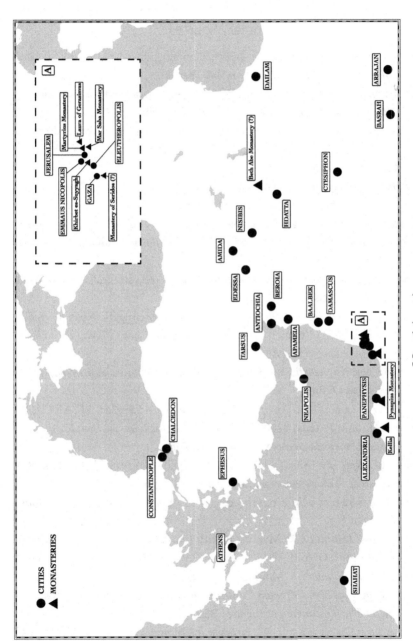

Map 1 (cont.)

Bibliography

Primary Sources

Acts of the Synod of Ephesus in 449 = Flemming, J. (ed.) (1917) *Akten der ephesinischen Synode vom Jahre 449*. Berlin.

Ammianus, *History* = Seyfarth, W. (ed. and trans.) (1968) *Ammianus Marcellinus: Römische Geschichte*, (4 vols) Leipzig.

Anthony, *Letters* = 'Translation of Letters', in: Rubenson, S. (ed. and trans.) (1995) *The Letters of St. Antony: Monasticism and the Making of a Saint*. Minneapolis, pp. 197–232.

Apophthegemata Patrum = Wortley, J. (ed. and trans.) (2013) *The 'Anonymous' Sayings of the Desert Fathers*. Cambridge.

Athanasius, *Letter to Virgins* = 'Second Letter to the Virgins', in D. Brakke (ed. and trans.) *Athanasius and the Politics of Asceticism*. Clarendon Press, pp. 292–302.

Athanasius, *Life of Anthony* = Bartelink, G.J.M. (ed. and trans.) (2004) *Vie d'Antoine*. Paris.

Barsanuphius and John, *Letters* = Neyt, F. and de Angelis-Noah, P. (ed.), Regnault, L. (trans.) (1997) *Barsanuphe et Jean de Gaza. Correspondance* (5 vols) Paris.

Basil of Caesarea, *Asketikon* = Silvas, A. (ed.) (2005) *The Asketikon of St Basil the Great*. Oxford.

Bede, *Ecclesiastical History of the English People* = Lapidge, M., Monat, P., and Robin, P. (eds) (2005) *Histoire Ecclésiastique du Peuple Anglais. Historia ecclesiastica gentis Anglorum*. Paris.

Caesarius, *Rule for Nuns* = de Vogüé, A. and Courreau, J. (eds) (1988) *Caesarius. Œuvres monastiques*. Paris, Vol 2, pp. 170-272.

Caesarius, *Sermons* = Morin, G. (ed.) (1953) *Caesarius of Arles. Sermons*. Turnhout.

Cassiodorus, *Institutions* = Mynors, R.A.B. (ed.) (1937) *Cassiodori Senatoris Institutiones*. Oxford.

Codex Theodosianus = Mommsen, T. and Meyer, P.M. (eds) (1954) *Theodosiani libri XVI: cum Constitutionibus Sirmondianis et Leges novellae ad Theodosianum pertinentes*. Berlin.

Corpus Iuris Civilis = Kroll, W., Krueger, P., Mommsen, Th., Schöll, R. (eds) (1892) *Corpus iuris civilis* (3 vols) Berlin.

Cyril of Scythopolis, *Lives of the Monks of Palestine* = Eduard Schwartz (ed.) (1939) *Kyrillos von Skythopolis*, Leipzig, transl. in: Binns, J. (ed.) Price, R.M. (trans.) (1991) *Lives of the Monks of Palestine*. Kalamazoo.

Eucherius of Lyon, *In Praise of the Desert* = 'De Laude Eremi', in Migne, J.P. (ed.) (1846) *Patrologia Latina*, 50, Paris, cols. 701–712.

Evagrius Scholasticus, *Church History* = Hübner, A. (ed. and trans.) (2007) *Evagrius Scholasticus. Historia ecclesiastica – Kirchengeschichte*. Turnhout.

Fructuosus, *General rule* = 'General Rule for Monasteries', in Barlow, C.W. (ed. and trans.) (1969) *Iberian Fathers, Volume 2: Writings of Braulio of Saragossa and Fructuosus of Braga*. Washington.

Gerontius, *Life of Melania* = Laurence, P. (ed. and trans.) (2002) *La Vie Latine de Sainte Mélanie*. Jerusalem.

Gregory of Tours, *Histories* = Krusch, B. and Levison, W. (eds) (1951) 'Gregorii episcopi Turonensis. Libri Historiarum X', in MGH SRM I 1. Hannover.

Gregory of Tours, *Life of Monegundis* = de Nie, G. (ed. and trans.) (2015) *Lives and Miracles*. Cambridge, pp. 266–285.

Gregory of Tours, *Lives and Miracles* = de Nie, G. (trans.) (2015) *Lives and Miracles*. Cambridge.

Gregory the Great, *Letters* = Norberg, D. (ed.) (1982) *Epistulae*. Turnhout.

Historia monachorum in Aegypto = Festugière, A.J. (ed.) (1961) *Historia monachorum in Aegypto*. Bruxelles.

Isidore, *Etymologiae* = Barney S. A., Lewis, W. J., Beach, J. A., Berghof, O. (ed. and trans.) (2006). *The Etymologies of Isidore of Seville*. Cambridge.

Iso'dnah, *The Book of Chastity* = Chabot, J.-B. (ed. and trans.) (1896) *Le Livre de la Chasteté*. Rome.

Iso'yahb III, *Letters* = Duval, R. (ed. and trans.) (1904) *Iso'yahb III Patriarcha: Liber epistularum* (2 vols) Leipzig.

Jerome, *Letters* = Hilberg, I. (ed.) (1912) *Hieronymus Epistulae*. Leipzig.

Jerome, *Life of Hilarion* = 'Vita Sancti Hilarionis', in Migne, J.P. (ed.) (1844) *Patrologia Latina*, 23, Paris, pp. 29–55.

John Cassian, *The Conferences* = Pichery, E. (ed.) (1955) *Collationes Patrum*. Paris.

John Malalas, *Chronicle* = Thurn, H. (ed.) (2000) *Ioannis Malalae Chronographia*. Berlin.

John Moschus, *The Spiritual Meadow* = Rouët de Journel, M.J. (ed.) (2006) *Le Pré Spirituel*. Paris. Translated in Wortley J. (trans.) (1992) *The Spiritual Meadow*. Kalamazoo.

Jonas of Bobbio, *Life of Columbanus* = 'Vita Columbani' in: Krusch B. (ed.) (1905) MGH SS rer. Germ. 37, Hannover, pp. 1–294.

Julianus Pomerius, *The Contemplative Life* = 'De Vita Contemplativa' in Migne, J.P. (ed.) (1850) *Patrologia Latina*, 59. Paris, col. 415-520.

Leontios of Napolis, *Life of St John the Almsgiver* = Gelzer, H. (ed.) (1893) *Leontios' von Neapolis Leben des Heiligen Johannes des Barmherzigen Erzbishofs von Alexandrien*. Freiburg.

Libanius, Orations = 'Orationes' in Foerster, R. (ed.) (1903-1908) *Libanii opera omnia*. Vols 1–4. Leipzig.

Life of Caesarius = Delage, M.-J. (ed.) (2010) *Vie de Césaire d'Arles*. Paris.

Life of John of Dailam = Brock, S.P. (1981) 'A Syriac Life of John of Dailam', *Parole de l'Orient* 10, pp. 123–89.

Life of Lupicinus = Martine, F. (ed.) (2004) *Vie des Pères du Jura*. Paris, pp. 308–363.

Life of Onnophrius = 'Life of Onnophrius', in Wallis Budge, E.A. (ed.) (1914) *Coptic Martyrdoms etc. in the Dialect of Upper Egypt*. New York, pp. 205–224.

Life of Pachomius = Halkin, F. (ed.) (1932) *Sancti Pacomii Vitae Graecae*. Bruxelles.

Life of Rabbula = 'Vita', in: Overbeck, J.J. (ed.) (1865) *S. Ephraemi Syri, Rabulae episcopi Edesseni, Balaei aliorumque opera selecta, e codicibus Syriacis manuscriptis in Museo Britannico et Bibliotheca Bodleiana asservatis primus edidit*. Oxford, pp. 159–209.

Life of Rusticula = 'Vita Rusticulae sive Marciae abbatissae Arelatensis', in Krusch, B. (ed.) (1902) MGH SRM 4. Hannover, pp. 339–351.

Lives of the Jura Fathers = Martine, F. (ed.) (2004) *Vie des pères du Jura*. Paris.

Marius of Avenches, *Chronicle* = Favrod, J. (ed. and trans.) (1993) *La chronique de Marius d'Avenches*: 455 - 581. Lausanne.

Met 14.1.140 = Crum, W.E. and Evelyn White, H. (eds) (1926) *The Monastery of Epiphanius at Thebes: Part II, Coptic Ostraca and Papyri*. New York, p. 320.

MGH DRF = Kölzer, T. (ed.) (2001) *Die Urkunden der Merowinger* (2 vols). Hannover.

Palladius, *Dialogue on the Life of John Chrysostom* = Malingrey, A. -M. and Leclercq P. (eds) (1988) *Dialogue sur la Vie de Jean Chrysostome*, 2 vols. Paris.

Palladius, *The Lausiac History* = Butler C. (ed.) (1904) *The Lausiac history of Palladius*, Vol. 2. Cambridge.

Paulinus of Nola, *Letters* = Hartel, G. (ed.) (1894) *Paulinus Nolanus Epistulae.* Vienna.

Procopius, *Wars* = Haury, J. (ed.), Wirth, G. (rev.) (1962) *History of the Wars.* Leipzig.

Rabbula, *Adm. Mon.* = 'Monita ad Coenobitas' in Overbeck, J.J. (ed.) (1865) *S. Ephraemi Syri, Rabulae episcopi Edesseni, Balaei aliorumque opera selecta, e codicibus Syriacis manuscriptis in Museo Britannico et Bibliotheca Bodleiana asservatis primus edidit.* Oxford, pp. 212–214.

Rule of Augustine = Verheijen, L. (ed.) (1967) *La Règle de Saint Augustin.* Vol. 1. Paris, pp. 105–107.

Ruricius, *Letters* = 'Ruricii Epistolae' in Krusch, B. (ed.) (1887) MGH Auct. ant. 8. Berlin, pp. 299–350.

Shenoute, *Rules* = 'The Rules, Edited and Translated' in: Layton, B. (ed. and trans.) (2014) *The Canons of Our Fathers: monastic rules of Shenoute.* Oxford, pp. 92–342.

Sophronius of Jerusalem, *Life of Mary* = 'The Life of Mary of Egypt', in Talbot, A.-M. (ed.) and Kouli, M. (trans.) (1996) *Holy Women of Byzantium: Ten Saints' Lives in English* Translation. Washington, pp. 65–95.

Sozomen, *Historia ecclesiastica* = Hansen, G.C. (ed. and trans.) (2004) *Sozomenos. Historia Ecclesiastica – Kirchengeschichte.* Turnhout.

Sulpicius Severus, *Life of St Martin* = Burton, P. (ed. and trans.) (2017) *Sulpicius Severus' Vita Martini.* Oxford.

Synesius, *Letters* = Lacombrade, C., Garzya, A., Lamoureux, J. (eds) (1978) *Synésios de Cyrène*, Vol 2–3: *Correspondance.* Paris.

The Acts of the Lateran Synod of 649 = Rudolf, R. (ed.) (1984) *Concilium Lateranense a. 649 celebratum.* Berlin.

The Rule of Benedict = Vogüé, A. de and Neufville, J. (eds and trans) (1971) *La Règle de Saint Benoît.* Paris.

The Rules of the Fathers = Vogüé, A. de (ed. and trans.) (1982) *Les Règles des Saints Pères.* 2 vols. Paris.

The Statutes of the School of Nisibis = Vööbus, A. (ed.) (1961) *The Statutes of the School of Nisibis.* Stockholm.

The Synod of Mar Acacius = 'The Synod of Mar Acacius', in Chabot, J.B. (ed. and trans.) (1902a) *Synodicon orientale ou recueil de synodes nestoriens.* Paris, pp. 299–307.

The Synod of Mar Joseph = 'The Synod of Mar Joseph', in Chabot, J.B. (ed. and trans.) (1902b) *Synodicon orientale ou recueil de synodes nestoriens*. Paris, pp. 352–367.

Theoderet, *History of the Monks* = Canivet, P. and Leroy-Molinghen, A. (eds and trans) (1977) *Histoire des moines de Syrie: Histoire Philothée*. Paris.

Valerius of Bierzo, *Ordo Querimoniae; Replicatio; Residuum* = Aherne, C.M. (ed.) (1949) *Valerio of Bierzo: An ascetic of the late Visigothic period*. Washington.

Secondary Literature

Bailey, L. (2006) 'Monks and Lay Communities in Late Antique Gaul: The Evidence of the Eusebius Gallicanus Sermons', *Journal of Medieval History*, 32(4), pp. 315–32.

Barat, K. (2002) 'Aluoben, a Nestorian Missionary in 7th Century China', *Journal of Asian History*, 36(2), pp. 184–98.

Basquin-Matthey, C. (2015) 'Les Exorcismes dans la Vie d'Hilarion: entre Intertextualité et Originalité', *Revue des Sciences Religieuses*, 89(2), pp. 165–84.

Beach, A. I. and Cochelin, I. (eds) (2020) *The Cambridge History of Medieval Monasticism in the Latin West*. Cambridge.

Becker, A. H. (2006) *Fear of God and the Beginning of Wisdom: The School of Nisibis and the Development of Scholastic Culture in Late Antique Mesopotamia*. Philadelphia.

Blanke, L. (2019) *An Archaeology of Egyptian Monasticism: Settlement, Economy and Daily Life at the White Monastery Federation*. Yale.

(2020) 'Pricing Salvation: Visitation, Donation and the Monastic Economies in Late Antique and Early Islamic Egypt', in Collar, A. and Kristensen, T. M. (eds) *Pilgrimage and Economy in the Ancient Mediterranean*. Leiden, pp. 228–53.

Bloch, H. (1987) 'Origin and Fate of the Bronze Doors of Abbot Desiderius of Monte Cassino', *Dumbarton Oaks Papers*, 41, pp. 89–102.

Bowes, K. (2011) 'Inventing Ascetic Space: Houses, Monasteries and the Archaeology of Asceticism', in Dey, H. and Fentress, E. (eds) *Western Monasticism Ante Litteram: The Spaces of Monastic Observance in Late Antiquity and the Early Middle Ages*. Turnhout, pp. 315–51.

Brakke, D. (1995) *Athanasius and the Politics of Asceticism*. Oxford.

Brennecke, H. C. (2014) 'Introduction: Framing the Historical and Theological Problems', in Berndt, G. and Steinacher, R. (eds) *Arianism: Roman Heresy and Barbarian Creed*. Farnham, pp. 1–20.

Bridge, G. and Watson, S. (2000) 'City Imaginaries', in Bridge, G. and Watson, S. (eds) *A Companion to the City*. Oxford, pp. 7–17.

Brock, S. P. (1981–2) 'A Syriac Life of John of Dailam', *Parole de l'Orient*, 10, pp. 123–89.

Brooks Hedstrom, D. L. (2017) *The Monastic Landscape of Late Antique Egypt*. Cambridge.

Brown, P. (1971) 'The Rise and Function of the Holy Man in Late Antiquity', *The Journal of Roman Studies*, 61, pp. 80–101.

(1978) *The World of Late Antiquity: AD 150–750*. Harvard.

(1988) *The Body and Society: Men, Women and Sexual Renunciation in Early Christianity*. London.

(2003) *The Rise of Western Christendom: Triumph and Diversity, AD 750–1250*, 2nd ed. Cambridge, MA.

(2005) 'Augustine and a Crisis of Wealth in Late Antiquity: University of Villanova, Saint Augustine Lecture 2004', *Augustinian Studies*, 36(1), pp. 5–30.

(2013) *Through the Eye of a Needle: Wealth, the Fall of Rome, and the Making of Christianity in the West, 350–550 AD*. Princeton.

(2015) *The Ransom of the Soul: Afterlife and Wealth in Early Western Christianity*. Cambridge.

Brown, R. H. (1987) *Society as Text: Essays on Rhetoric, Reason, and Reality*. Chicago.

Bruning, B. (2001) 'Otium and Negotium Within the One Church', *Augustiniana*, 51(1/2), pp. 105–149.

Bully, S., Bully, A., Čaušević-Bully, M., and Fiocchi, L. (2014) 'Les Origines du Monastère de Luxeuil (Haute-Saône) d'après les Récentes Recherches Archéologiques', in Gaillard, M. (ed.) *L'Empreinte Chrétienne en Gaule du IVè au IXè Siècle*. Turnhout, pp. 311–56.

Bully, S., Destefanis, E. and Marron, E. (2020) 'The Archaeology of the Earliest Monasteries in Italy and France (Second Half of the Fourth Century to the Eighth Century)', in Beach, A. I. and Cochelin, I. (eds) *The Cambridge History of Medieval Monasticism in the Latin West*. Cambridge, pp. 232–57.

Burrus, V. (1995) *The Making of a Heretic: Gender, Authority, and the Priscillianist Controversy*. Berkeley.

Cain, A. (2016) *The Greek Historia Monachorum in Aegypto: Monastic Hagiography in the Late Fourth Century*. Oxford.

Cameron, A. (1976) *Circus Factions, Blues and Greens at Rome and Constantinople*. Oxford.

Camplani, A. (2007) 'The Revival of Persian Monasticism (Sixth to Seventh Centuries): Church Structures, Theological Academy, and Reformed Monks', in Camplani, A. and Filoramo, G. (eds) *Foundations of Power and Conflicts of Authority in Late-Antique Monasticism*. Leuven, pp. 277–96.

Canepa, M. P. (2018) *Iranian Expanse: Transforming Royal Identity through Architecture, Landscape, and the Built Environment, 550 BCE–642 CE*. Oakland.

Caner, D. (2002) *Wandering, Begging Monks: Spiritual Authority and the Promotion of Monasticism in Late Antiquity*. Berkeley.

Cartwright, S. (2016) 'Athanasius' "Vita Antonii" as Political Theology: The Call of Heavenly Citizenship', *The Journal of Ecclesiastical History*, 67 (2), pp. 241–64.

Charles-Edwards, T. M. (2000) *Early Christian Ireland*. Cambridge.

Chin, C. M. and Schroeder, C. T. (2016) *Melania: Early Christianity through the Life of One Family*. Berkeley.

Chitty, D. J. (1966) *The Desert a City*. Crestwood.

Clark, E. A. (2020) *Melania the Younger: From Rome to Jerusalem*. Oxford.

Codou, Y. and Lauwers, M. (2009) *Lérins, une Île Sainte dans l'Occident Médiéval*. Turnhout.

Collins, R. (1992) 'The "Autobiographical" Works of Valerius of Bierzo: Their Structure and Purpose', in Collins, R. (ed.) *Law, Culture and Regionalism in Early Medieval Spain*. Aldershot, pp. 425–42.

Coon, L. L. (1997) *Sacred Fictions: Holy Women and Hagiography in Late Antiquity*. Philadelphia.

Cooper, K. (2005) 'The Household and the Desert: Monastic and Biological Communities in the Lives of Melania the Younger', in Mulder-Bakker, A. B. and Wogan-Browne, J. (eds) *Household, Women, and Christianities in Late Antiquity and the Middle Ages*. Turnhout, pp. 11–36.

(2007a) 'Poverty, Obligation, Inheritance: Roman Heiresses and the Varieties of Senatorial Christianity in Fifth-Century Rome', in Cooper, K. and Hillner, J. (eds) *Religion, Dynasty and Patronage in Early Christian Rome 300–900*. Cambridge, pp. 165–89.

(2007b) *The Fall of the Roman Household*. Cambridge.

Cribiore, R. (1996) *Writing, Teachers, and Students in Graeco-Roman Egypt*. Atlanta.

(2007) *The School of Libanius in Late Antique Antioch*. Princeton.

Crislip, A. T. (2005) *From Monastery to Hospital: Christian Monasticism & the Transformation of Health Care in Late Antiquity*. Ann Arbor.

Dailey, E. T. (2015) *Queens, Consorts, Concubines: Gregory of Tours and Women of the Merovingian Elite*. Leiden.

Demacopoulos, G. E. (2015) *Gregory the Great: Ascetic, Pastor, and First Man of Rome*. Notre Dame.

Diaz, P. C. (2018) 'Discipline and Punishment in 7th Century Visigothic Monasticism: The Contrast between Isidore's and Fructuosus' Rules', in Alciati, R. (ed.) *Norm and Exercise: Christian Asceticism between Late Antiquity and Early Middle Ages*. Stuttgart, pp. 107–23.

Diem, A. (2013) 'The Gender of the Religious: Wo/men and the Invention of Monasticism', in Benett, J. M. and Karras, R. M. (eds) *The Oxford Handbook of Women and Gender in Medieval Europe*. Oxford, pp. 432–46.

(2019) 'The Limitations of Asceticism', *Medieval Worlds*, (9), pp. 112–38.

(2021) *The Pursuit of Salvation: Community, Space, and Discipline in Early Medieval Monasticism: With a Critical Edition and Translation of the Regula cuiusdam ad uirgines*. Turnhout.

Diem, A. and Rousseau, P. (2020) 'Monastic Rules (Fourth to Ninth Century)', in Beach, A. I. and Cochelin, I. (eds) *The Cambridge History of Medieval Monasticism in the Latin West*. Cambridge, pp. 162–94.

Diniz, L. R. G. (2021) 'Valerius of Bierzo as an Interpreter of the Seventh-Century Ecclesiastical Environment of Northwestern Iberia', *Journal of Medieval Iberian Studies*, 13(2), pp. 145–63.

Doherty, C. (1985) 'The Monastic Town in Early Medieval Ireland', in Clarke, H. B. and Simms, A. (eds) *The Comparative History of Urban Origins in Non-Roman Europe: Ireland, Wales, Denmark, Germany, Poland and Russia from the 9th to the 13th Century*. Oxford, pp. 45–75.

Drijvers, J. W. (1996) 'The Man of God of Edessa, Bishop Rabbula, and the Urban Poor: Church and Society in the Fifth Century', *Journal of Early Christian Studies*, 4(2), pp. 235–48.

Dunn, M. (2000) *The Emergence of Monasticism: From the Desert Fathers to the Early Middle Ages*. Oxford.

Elm, E. (2020) 'Hilarion and the Bactrian Camel: Demons and Genre in Jerome's Life of Hilarion', in Elm, E. and Hartmann, N. (eds) *Demons in Late Antiquity: Their Perception and Transformation in Different Literary Genres*. Berlin, pp. 119–34.

Elm, S. (1994) *'Virgins of God': The Making of Asceticism in Late Antiquity* Oxford.

(1998) 'The Dog that Did Not Bark: Doctrine and Patriarchal Authority in the Conflict between Theophilus of Alexandria and John Chrysostom of Constantinople', in Ayres, L. and Jones, G. (eds) *Christian Origins: Theology, Rhetoric and Community*. London, pp. 68–93.

Etchingham, C. (2002) *Church Organisation in Ireland AD 650 to 1000*. Maynooth.

Fafinski, M. and Riemenschneider, J. (2022) 'Literarised Spaces: Towards a Narratological Framework for Late Antiquity and the Early Middle Ages', in Fafinski, M. and Riemenschneider, J. (eds) *The Past through Narratology: New Approaches to Late Antiquity and the Early Middle Ages*. Heidelberg, pp. 7–23.

Fick, P. H. (2011) 'Traces of Augustinian 'Gnosis' in Julianus Pomerius *De vita contemplativa*', in van den Berg, J. A., Kotzé A., Nicklas, T., and Scopello, M. (eds) *'In Search of the Truth': Augustine, Manicheism, and other Gnosticisim: Studies for Johannes von Oort at Sixty*. Leiden, pp. 189–98.

Finneran, N. (2012) 'Hermits, Saints, and Snakes: The Archaeology of the Early Ethiopian Monastery in Wider Context', *The International Journal of African Historical Studies*, 45(2), pp. 247–71.

Gaube, H. (1986) 'Arrajan', in Yarshater, E. (ed.) *Encyclopaedia Iranica*, vol. 2, fasc. 5. London, pp. 519–20.

Goddard, C. J. (2021) 'Euergetism, Christianity and Municipal Culture in Late Antiquity, from Aquileia to Gerasa (Fourth to Sixth Centuries CE)', in Zuiderhoek, A. and Domingo Gygax, M. (eds) *Benefactors and the Polis: The Public Gift in the Greek Cities from the Homeric World to Late Antiquity*. Cambridge, pp. 297–329.

Goehring, J. E. (1993) 'The Encroaching Desert: Literary Production and Ascetic Space in Early Christian Egypt', *Journal of Early Christian Studies*, 1, pp. 281–96.

(1996) 'Withdrawing from the Desert: Pachomius and the Development of Village Monasticism in Upper Egypt', *The Harvard Theological Review*, 89, pp. 267–85.

(1999) *Ascetics, Society, and the Desert*. Harrisburg.

(2003) 'The Dark Side of Landscape: Ideology and Power in the Christian Myth of the Desert', *The Journal of Medieval and Early Modern Studies*, 33, pp. 437–51.

Goodrich, R. J. (2007) *Contextualizing Cassian: Aristocrats, Asceticism, and Reformation in Fifth-Century Gaul*. Oxford.

Grig, L. (2013) 'Cities in the "Long" Late Antiquity, 2000–2012: A Survey Essay', *Urban History*, 40(3), pp. 554–66.

Guidetti, M. (2009) 'The Byzantine Heritage in the Dār Al-Islām: Churches and Mosques in Al-Ruha between the Sixth and Twelfth Centuries', *Muqarnas*, 26, pp. 1–36.

Guillaumont, A. Coquin, R. - G., Weidmann, D., Grossmann, P., Partyka, J. S. and Rassart-Debergh, M. (1991) 'Kellia', *The Coptic Encyclopedia.*, New York, 5, pp. 1396b–410a.

Hammer, C. I. (2012) *Town and Country in Early-Medieval Bavaria: Two Studies in Urban and Comital Structure*. Oxford.

Hasse-Ungeheuer, A. (2016) *Das Mönchtum in der Religionspolitik Kaiser Justinians I: Die Engel des Himmels und der Stellvertreter Gottes auf Erden*. Berlin.

Hatlie, P. (2006) 'Monks and Circus Factions in Early Byzantine Political Life', in Kaplan, M. (ed.) *Monastères, Images, Pouvoirs et Société à Byzance*. Paris, pp. 13–25.

Hemelrijk, E. A. (2004) 'Patronage of Cities: The Role of Women', in De Ligt, L., Hemelrijk, E., and Singor, H. W. (eds) *Roman Rule and Civic Life: Local and Regional Perspectives*. Leiden, pp. 415–27.

Henning, J. (2007) 'Early European Towns: The Way of the Economy in the Frankish Area between Dynamism and Deceleration 500–1000 AD', in Henning, J. (ed.) *Post-Roman Towns, Trade and Settlement in Europe and Byzantium*. Berlin, pp. 3–40.

Hevelone-Harper, J. L. (2016) 'The Letter Collection of Barsanuphius and John', in Sogno, C., Storin, B. K., and Watts, E. J. (eds) *Late Antique Letter Collections: A Critical Introduction and Reference Guide*. Berkeley, pp. 418–32.

Hirschfeld, Y. (1992) *The Judean Desert Monasteries in the Byzantine Period*. New Haven.

Hose, M. (2019) 'The Importance of the Greek Polis for Greek Literature, or Why Gaza?', in Stenger, J. R. (ed.) *Learning Cities in Late Antiquity: The Local Dimension of Education*. London, pp. 47–69.

Humphries, M. (2019) Cities and the Meanings of Late Antiquity. Leiden: Brill.

Hunter, E. C. D. (2012) 'Syriac, Sogdian and Old Uyghur Manuscripts from Bulayïq', in Academia Turfanica (ed.) *The History Behind the Languages: Essays of the Turfan Forum on Old Languages of the Silk Road [*語言背後的歷史—西域古典語言學高峰論壇論文集*]*. Shanghai, pp. 79–93.

(2021) 'Turfan: Connecting with Seleucia-Ctesiphon', *Entangled Religions*, 11(6).

Ioan, O. (2009) *Muslime und Araber bei Īšōʿjahb III. (649–659)*. Wiesbaden.

Isola, A. (2006) '"De monachis" un Titolo Controverso (codex Theodosianus 16, 3, 1/2)', *Wiener Studien*, 119, pp. 199–214.

Izdebski, A. (2019) 'Biskupi i mnisi w Kościele Wschodu pod panowaniem Sasanidów (=Bishops and Monks in the Church of the East in the Sassanian Period)', *U Schyłku Starożytności: studia źródłoznawcze*, (17/18), pp. 171–96.

Jones, A. E. (2009) *Social Mobility in Late Antique Gaul: Strategies and Opportunities for the Non-Elite*. Cambridge.

Jones, A. H. M. (1965) *The Decline of the Ancient World*. London.

Klein, W. (2004) 'A Newly Excavated Church of Syriac Christianity along the Silk Road in Kyrghyzstan', *The Journal of Eastern Christian Studies*, 56, pp. 25–47.

Klingshirn, W. E. (1994) *Caesarius of Arles: The Making of a Christian Community in Late Antique Gaul.* Cambridge.

Larsen, L. and Rubenson, S. (eds) (2018) *Monastic Education in Late Antiquity: The Transformation of Classical 'Paideia'.* Cambridge.

Layton, R. A. (2004) *Didymus the Blind and His Circle in Late-Antique Alexandria: Virtue and Narrative in Biblical Scholarship.* Urbana.

Leppin, H. (2020) 'Creating a City of Believers: Rabbula of Edessa', in Lätzer-Lasar, A. and Urciuoli, E. R. (eds) *Urban Religion in Late Antiquity.* Berlin, pp. 185–204.

Letsch-Brunner, S. (1998) *Marcella – discipula et magistra: auf den Spuren einer Römischen Christin des 4. Jahrhunderts.* Berlin.

Leyser, C. (1991) *The Monastic Thought and Culture of Pope Gregory the Great in their Western Context, c.400–604.* University of Oxford. https://ora.ox.ac.uk/objects/uuid:a8280d1b-1d09-4505-ad0d-2be735badbaf (Accessed 10 November 2022).

(2000) *Authority and Asceticism from Augustine to Gregory the Great.* Oxford.

(2006) 'The Uses of the Desert in the Sixth-Century West', *Church History and Religious Culture*, 86(1/4), pp. 113–34.

Liebeschuetz, J. W. (2001) *Decline and Fall of the Roman City.* Oxford.

Lillington-Martin, C. and Turquois, É. (eds) (2017) *Procopius of Caesarea: Literary and Historical Interpretations.* London.

Livne-Kafri, O. (1996) 'Early Muslim Ascetics and the World of Christian Monasticism', *Jerusalem Studies in Arabic and Islam*, 20, pp. 105–29.

Maas, M. (2003) *Exegesis and Empire in the Early Byzantine Mediterranean: Junillus Africanus and the 'Instituta regularia divinae legis'.* Tübingen.

Maravela, A. (2018) 'Homer and Menandri Sententiae in Upper Egyptian Monastic Settings', in Larsen, L. I. and Rubenson, S. (eds) *Monastic Education in Late Antiquity: The Transformation of Classical Paideia.* Cambridge, pp. 125–50.

Markus, R. A. (1981) 'Gregory the Great's Europe', *Transactions of the Royal Historical Society*, 31, pp. 21–36.

(1997) *Gregory the Great and His World.* Cambridge.

Martin, C. (2017–18) 'The Asturia of Valerius: Bierzo at the End of the Seventh Century', *Visigothic Symposium*, 2, pp. 60–78.

McCormick, M. (2001) *Origins of the European Economy: Communications and Commerce AD 300–900.* Cambridge.

McKitterick, R. (1979) 'Town and Monastery in the Carolingian Period', *Studies in Church History*, 16, pp. 93–102.

Melucci, A. (1996) *Challenging Codes: Collective Action in the Information Age*. Cambridge.

Meyvaert, P. (1994) 'Bede and Gregory the Great', in Lapidge, M. (ed.) *Bede and His World: The Jarrow Lectures*. London, pp. 103–32.

(1996) 'Bede, Cassiodorus and the Codex Amiatinus', *Speculum*, 71, pp. 827–83.

Michałowski, K. (1967) *Faras, die Kathedrale aus dem Wüstensand*. Einsiedeln.

Morony, M. G. (1974) 'Religious Communities in Late Sasanian and Early Muslim Iraq', *Journal of the Economic and Social History of the Orient*, 17 (2), pp. 113–35.

Muehlberger, E. (2015) 'Simeon and Other Women in Theodoret's Religious History: Gender in the Representation of Late Ancient Christian Asceticism', *Journal of Early Christian Studies*, 23(4), pp. 583–606.

Nicolini-Zani, M. (2009) 'The Tang Christian Pillar from Luoyang and its Jingjiao Inscription: A Preliminary Study', *Monumenta Serica*, 57, pp. 99–140.

(2013) 'Luminous Ministers of the Da Qin Monastery: A Study of the Christian Clergy Mentioned in the Jingjiao Pillar from Luoyang', in Tang, L. and Winkler, D. W. (eds) *From the Oxus River to the Chinese Shores: Studies on East Syriac Christianity in China and Central Asia*. Berlin, pp. 141–60.

Ó Carragáin, T. (2015) 'Is there an Archaeology of Lay People at Early Irish Monasteries?', in Bully, S. and Sapin, C. (eds) *Au Seuil du Cloître: la Présence des Laïcs (Hôtelleries, Bâtiments d'Accueil, Activités Artisanales et de Services) entre le Ve et le XIIe Siècle*. Auxerre.

Obłuski, A. (2019) *The Monasteries and Monks of Nubia*. Warsaw.

Oexle, O. G. (2011) 'Koinos bios: Die Entstehung des Mönchtums', in Oexle, O. G. Jussen, B., Hülsen-Esch, A. von, and Rexroth, F. (eds) *Die Wirklichkeit und das Wissen: Mittelalterforschung, historische Kulturwissenschaft, Geschichte und Theorie der historischen Erkenntnis*. Göttingen, pp. 470–95.

Patrich, J. (2001) 'The Sabaite Heritage: An Introductory Survey', in Patrich, J. (ed.) *The Sabaite Heritage in the Orthodox Church from the Fifth Century to the Present*. Leuven, pp. 1–27.

Payne, R. E. (2015) *A State of Mixture: Christians, Zoroastrians, and Iranian Political Culture in Late Antiquity*. Oxford.

Percival, J. (1997) 'Villas and Monasteries in Late Roman Gaul', *The Journal of Ecclesiastical History*, 48(1), pp. 1–21.

Phenix, R. R. and Horn, C. B. (2017) *The Rabbula Corpus: Comprising the Life of Rabbula, His Correspondence, a Homily Delivered in Constantinople, Canons, and Hymns*. Atlanta.

Pollheimer, M. (2015) 'Divine Law and Imperial Rule: The Carolingian Reception of Junillus Africanus', in Gantner, C., McKitterick, R., and Meeder, S. (eds) *The Resources of the Past in Early Medieval Europe*. Cambridge, pp. 118–34.

Rapp, C. (2006) 'Desert, City, and Countryside in the Early Christian Imagination', in Dijkstra, J. and van Dijk, H. (eds) *The Encroaching Desert: Egyptian Hagiography and the Medieval West*. Leiden, pp. 93–112.

(2019) 'Monastic Jargon and Citizenship Language in Late Antiquity', *Al-Masaq*, 32(1), pp. 54–63.

Rebenich, S. R. (2002) *Jerome*. London.

Reinink, G. J. (1995) 'Edessa Grew Dim and Nisibis Shone Forth: The School of Nisisbis at the Transition of the Sixth-Seventh Century', in Drijvers, J. W. and MacDonald, A. A. (eds) *Centres of Learning: Learning and Location in Pre-modern Europe and the Near East*. Leiden, pp. 77–89.

Rousseau, P. (1978) *Ascetics, Authority, and the Church in the Age of Jerome and Cassian*, 2nd ed. Notre Dame.

Rubenson, S. (2013) 'The Formation and Re-formations of the Sayings of the Desert Fathers', *Studia Patristica*, 55(3), pp. 5–22.

Salvesen, A. (2008) 'Jacob of Edessa's Life and Work: A Biographical Sketch', in Romeny, B. T. H. (ed.) *Jacob of Edessa and the Syriac Culture of His Day*. Leiden, pp. 1–10.

Salway, R. and Drinkwater, J. (2007) *Wolf Liebeschuetz Reflected*. London.

Salzman, M. R. (2017) 'From a Classical to a Christian City: Civic Euergetism and Charity in Late Antique Rome', *Studies in Late Antiquity*, 1(1), pp. 65–85.

Santangeli Valenzani, R. (1994) 'Tra la Porticus Minucia e il Calcarario: l'Area Sacra di Largo Argentina nell'Altomedioevo', *Archeologia Medievale*, 21, pp. 57–98.

Scheidel, W. (1999) 'Emperors, Aristocrats, and the Grim-Reaper: Towards a Demographic Profile of the Roman Elite', *Classical Quarterly*, 49(1), pp. 254–81.

Schlange-Schöningen, H. (2018) *Hieronymus: eine Historische Biografie*. Darmstadt.

Simpson, S. J. (2017) 'Sasanian Cities: Archaeological Perspectives on the Urban Economy and Built Environment of an Empire', in Sauer, E. (ed.)

Sasanian Persia: Between Rome and the Steppes of Eurasia. Edinburgh, pp. 21–50.

Stefaniw, B. (2018) 'The School of Didymus the Blind in Light of the Tura Find', in Larsen, L. I. and Rubenson, S. (eds) *Monastic Education in Late Antiquity: The Transformation of Classical Paideia*. Cambridge, pp. 153–81.

Swift, C. (1998) 'Forts and Fields: Study of "Monastic Towns" in Seventh and Eighth Century Ireland', *The Journal of Irish Archaeology*, 9, pp. 105–25.

Tanaseanu-Döbler, I. (2008) *Konversion zur Philosophie in der Spätantike: Kaiser Julian und Synesios von Kyrene*. Stuttgart.

Tannous, J. (2018) *The Making of the Medieval Middle East: Religion, Society, and Simple Believers*. Princeton.

Taxel, I. (2009) *Khirbet es-Suyyagh: A Byzantine Monastery in the Judaean Shephelah*. Tel Aviv.

Tilley, M. (2018) 'Caesarius's Rule for Unruly Nuns: Permitted and Prohibited Textiles in the Monastery of St John', *Early Medieval Europe*, 26(1), pp. 83–9.

Tutty, P. (2017) 'The Political and Philanthropic Role of Monastic Figures and Monasteries as Revealed in Fourth-Century Coptic and Greek Correspondence', *Studia patristica*, 91, pp. 353–62.

Tzaferis, V. (2001) 'Early Christian Monasticism in the Holy Land and Archaeology', in Patrich, J. (ed.) *The Sabaite Heritage in the Orthodox Church from the Fifth Century to the Present*. Leuven, pp. 317–21.

Valverde Castro, M. D. R. (2011) 'La Monarquía Visigoda en Valerio del Bierzo', *Edad Media: Revista de historia*, 12, pp. 281–300.

Vanderputten, S. (2020) *Medieval Monasticisms: Forms and Experiences of the Monastic Life in the Latin West*. München.

Vanderspoel, J. (1990) 'Cassiodorus as patricius and ex patricio', *Historia: Zeitschrift für Alte Geschichte*, 39, pp. 499–503.

Veyne, P. (1976) *Le Pain et le Cirque: Sociologie Historique d'un Pluralisme Politique*. Paris.

Vööbus, A. (1965) *History of the School of Nisibis*. Louvain.

Ward-Perkins, B. (2000) 'Constantinople: A City and its Ideological Territory', in Brogiolo, G. P., Gauthier, N., and Christie, N. (eds) *Towns and their Territories between Late Antiquity and the Early Middle Ages*. Leiden, pp. 325–45.

Watts, E. J. (2010) *Riot in Alexandria: Tradition and Group Dynamics in Late Antique Pagan and Christian Communities*. Berkeley.

Weiss, Z. (2014) Public Spectacles in Roman and Late Antique Palestine. Cambridge.

Westergren, A. (2018) 'The Monastic Paradox: Desert Ascetics as Founders, Fathers, and Benefactors in Early Christian Historiography', *Vigiliae Christianae*, 72(3), pp. 283–317.

Williams, M. H. (2006) *The Monk and the Book: Jerome and the Making of Christian Scholarship*. Chicago.

Wimbush, V. L. and Valantasis, R. (2002) *Asceticism*. Oxford.

Wipszycka, E. (2014) *Drugi dar Nilu*. Kraków.

(2018) 'The Canons of the Council of Chalcedon Concerning Monks', *Augustinianum*, 58(1), pp. 155–80.

Wojtczak, M. (2019) '"Legal Representation" of Monastic Communities in Late Antique Papyri', *Journal of Juristic Papyrology*, 49, pp. 347–99.

Wood, I. (2018) *The Transformation of the Roman West*. Leeds.

(2022) *The Christian Economy of the Early Medieval West: Towards a Temple Society*. Santa Barbara.

Wood, J. (2017) 'Monastic Space as Educative Space in Visigothic Iberia', *Visigothic Symposium*, 2, pp. 79–98.

Wood, P. J. (2013) *The Chronicle of Seert: Christian Historical Imagination in Late Antique Iraq*. Oxford.

Wood, S. (2006) *The Proprietary Church in the Medieval West*. Oxford.

Acknowledgements

This Element would never have been written if not for the help and encouragement of family, friends, and colleagues – it is impossible to thank them all enough. We would like to thank Andrew Jacobs for encouraging our initial ideas and guiding us through the process of writing and editing. Kate Cooper, Albrecht Diem, Michael Eber, Veronika Egetenmeyr, Stefan Esders, Rutger Kramer, and Roland Steinacher have read portions of this Element or whole drafts at various stages and their feedback has been invaluable. We would also like to especially thank our partners, Sarah Schlüssel and Anja Riemenschneider, for their patience and support – this Element is for them.

Cambridge Elements $\equiv$

Religion in Late Antiquity

Andrew S. Jacobs
Harvard Divinity School

Andrew S. Jacobs is Senior Fellow at the Center for the Study of World Religions at Harvard Divinity School. He has taught at the University of California, Riverside, Scripps College, and Harvard Divinity School and is the author of *Remains of the Jews: The Holy Land and Christian Empire in Late Antiquity; Christ Circumcised: A Study in Early Christian History and Difference;* and *Epiphanius of Cyprus: A Cultural Biography of Late Antiquity.* He has co-edited *Christianity in Late Antiquity, 300-450 C.E.: A Reader* and *Garb of Being: Embodiment and the Pursuit of Asceticism in Late Ancient Christianity.*

About the Series
This series brings a holistic and comparative approach to religious belief and practice from 100–800 C.E. throughout the Mediterranean and Near East. Volumes will explore the key themes that characterize religion in late antiquity and will often cross traditional disciplinary lines. The series will include contributions from classical studies, Early Christianity, Judaism, and Islam, among other fields.

Cambridge Elements ≡

Religion in Late Antiquity

Elements in the Series

Printed in the United States
by Baker & Taylor Publisher Services